The Wild Shores / AMERICA'S

By Tee Loftin Snell   *Photographs by* Walter Meayers Edward

PREPARED BY THE SPECIAL PUBLICATIONS DIVISION

BEGINNINGS

Paintings by Louis S. Glanzman   *Foreword by* Dr. David Mark Griffiths

NATIONAL GEOGRAPHIC SOCIETY, WASHINGTON, D. C.

THE WILD SHORES:
AMERICA'S BEGINNINGS
By TEE LOFTIN SNELL
National Geographic Staff
Photographs by WALTER MEAYERS EDWARDS
Paintings by LOUIS S. GLANZMAN

Published by
THE NATIONAL GEOGRAPHIC SOCIETY
GILBERT M. GROSVENOR, *President*
MELVIN M. PAYNE, *Chairman of the Board*
OWEN R. ANDERSON, *Executive Vice President*
ROBERT L. BREEDEN, *Vice President,*
    Publications and Educational Media
ANDREW H. BROWN, *Consulting Editor*
DR. DAVID MARK GRIFFITHS, *Consultant, Associate*
    Professor of History, University of North Carolina

Prepared by
THE SPECIAL PUBLICATIONS DIVISION
DONALD J. CRUMP, *Editor*
PHILIP B. SILCOTT, *Managing Editor*
MARJORIE W. CLINE, *Researcher*

Illustrations
WILLIAM L. ALLEN, *Picture Editor*
MARJORIE W. CLINE, GERALDINE LINDER,
    Illustrations Research
JAN NAGEL CLARKSON, JOHN S. GRAHAM,
    LOUIS DE LA HABA, MARGARET MCKELWAY
    JOHNSON, NATHANIEL T. KENNEY, LOUISA
    MAGZANIAN, TOM MELHAM, MARILYN L.
    WILBUR, *Picture Legends*

Design and Art Direction
JOSEPH A. TANEY, *Art Director*
JOSEPHINE B. BOLT, *Associate Art Director*
URSULA PERRIN, *Staff Designer*
Calligraphy by GUN LARSON

Production and Printing
ROBERT W. MESSER, *Production Manager*
GEORGE V. WHITE, *Assistant Production Manager*
RAJA D. MURSHED, NANCY W. GLASER, *Production*
    Assistants
JOHN R. METCALFE, *Engraving and Printing*
MARY G. BURNS, JANE H. BUXTON, MARTA
    ISABEL COONS, JANE M. D'ALELIO, TUCKER L.
    ETHERINGTON, SARA GROSVENOR, SUZANNE J.
    JACOBSON, SANDRA LEE MATTHEWS, JOAN PERRY,
    MARILYN L. WILBUR, KAREN G. WILSON, LINDA
    M. YEE, *Staff Assistants*
ANNE MCCAIN, PHILIP GUTEKUNST, *Index*

Second Printing 1983
Library of Congress CIP Data: page 203

*Overleaf: Coastline of Newfoundland, much as Europeans
saw it more than four and a half centuries ago, lies
under late-summer clouds. Settlements on the island slowly
grew around seasonal fishing stations of the 16th-century
fleets. Page 1: Roger Williams flees Massachusetts Bay
Colony in January 1636. Threatened with deportation for
preaching religious tolerance, he sought refuge among the
Indians. Front endpaper: From river trips in 1608,
John Smith drew this map of the Chesapeake Bay area.
Bookbinding: Indian chief, after John White. Back
endpaper: Map of New World settlements.*

OVERLEAF: SAM ABELL; PAGE 1: LOUIS S. GLANZMAN; FRONT ENDPAPER:
LIBRARY OF CONGRESS; BOOKBINDING: AFTER ENGRAVING BY THEO-
DORE DE BRY; BACK ENDPAPER: NATIONAL GEOGRAPHIC ART DIVISION.

SAM ABELL

*Newfoundlander hauls in a net heavy with
his catch. Harvested for centuries by fishing
fleets from many countries, the waters of
Newfoundland still abound with cod,
haddock, flounder, halibut, and capelin.*

Foreword

The first tenuous settlement at Jamestown...the long, perilous voyage of the tiny ship *Mayflower* to a wild and bleak landfall in Massachusetts....These dramatic events in the founding of the English colonies in America are familiar to most of us, if only in broad outline. Far less familiar, but equally dramatic, were the efforts of other maritime powers to stake their claims to the New World. The Vikings were first to arrive, but their brief stay left only a faint imprint on these shores. It was the later expeditions of such peoples as the Portuguese, Spanish, French, Dutch, Swedes, and Russians that contributed rich and enduring chapters to the story of America's early exploration and colonization.

The North American wilderness held out a variety of attractions to prospective settlers. For some, the new land offered the hope of material riches—gold, fish, furs. For others, it represented a haven where they could impose their own religious standards in an uncorrupted community. As the European presence became more firmly established, as summer camps gave way to year-round bases and then to permanent settlements, new colonists arrived whose interests lay in the more mundane pursuits of farming and trade.

However divergent the nationalities or motives of the early settlers, they all encountered common obstacles. Already physically and spiritually exhausted by the laborious ocean crossing, newcomers found a forbidding mainland guarded by rocky headlands, tangled forests, impenetrable swamps. Extremes in weather—paralyzing winters and searing summers—sometimes magnified the hardships. Along with the often harsh geography and climate, settlers had to contend with hostile natives who for the most part offered their cooperation only grudgingly, if at all.

But those who descended upon our shores were not of ordinary cloth. John Smith, Samuel de Champlain, Father Junípero Serra, Aleksandr Baranov—and those who accompanied them or followed them—possessed a venturesome spirit that released them from the restraints that bound the imaginations of ordinary people.

In this comprehensive and richly-illustrated volume, author Tee Loftin Snell brings these extraordinary individuals vividly to life. Through her carefully researched text, we learn their motives, follow their adventures, and share their hardships as they try to carve a future in the wilderness. More importantly, perhaps, we perceive an underlying love of freedom that would eventually shape the destiny of the continent and establish a new and independent nation.

DAVID MARK GRIFFITHS
Associate Professor of History
University of North Carolina

Portuguese ship under full sail approaches fishing waters off Newfoundland. John Cabot, exploring for England's King Henry VII, brought back news in 1497 of seas rich with cod. His report lured thousands of fishermen to the cold northern latitudes of the New World.

Contents

The Newfound Land

$\mathcal{D}$aring sea captain John Cabot brought the report all Bristol had hoped for during his 79-day absence. When his ship *Matthew* turned into England's cliff-walled Avon River on August 6, 1497, he doubtless shouted news of his discovery to the river pilots rowing out to meet him. A mounted messenger sped the magic words—Asia! Cathay!—eight miles upstream to Bristol.

Wealthy merchants who had invested in the voyage greeted Cabot, and many of the city's 10,000 people thronged the quay. Cabot told them of a shore hundreds of miles long that he had sailed past on the far western edge of the North Atlantic. Huge trees fit for great ships' masts covered much of that northern corner of "Asia," just three to four weeks' sail from Bristol. In offshore waters, he saw fish swimming so closely packed his men dipped them up in baskets.

It seemed that Italian John Cabot had discovered more for England than Italian Christopher Columbus had for Spain. Columbus had found for Queen Isabella and King Ferdinand only a scattering of islands 33 days or more west and south of the Canary Islands. And the Spanish had kept secret the details of the route.

Eyes fixed on the western horizon, a European voyager—a settler seeking land and possibly freedom from oppression—stands aboard a sailing ship, his hand resting on a mast shroud. A representation of a 16th-century map (background) shows ships under sail and a meeting of the Old World and the New.

17TH-CENTURY MARINER'S ASTROLABE (ABOVE)

Cabot, like Columbus, knew geography and navigation, and he was experienced as a Venetian spice merchant in the Levant. Using a globe he had made himself, he showed that far to the north of Columbus's islands lay the mainland his ship had touched. Although Cabot saw no cities, he was convinced that a few days' sail southwest along the coast would take him to the silks and spices of the Orient. King Henry VII agreed to help pay for Cabot's next trip. Joyfully, Bristol's merchants envisioned their ships hauling fortunes in luxuries to Europe. Bristol, not London or Seville, would gain the Far East trade that Venice had lost when Turks blocked the routes of the camel caravans.

Nearly 500 years after Cabot had leaped jubilantly onto Bristol's crowded quay, I jetted in a few hours across the North Atlantic to see his adopted city. There I began my search for stories of Cabot's discovery of the mainland and of the first people to try settling its wild shores over the next three centuries. Explorers would find that the northern continent was linked to another in the south. Without a break, the great land masses stretched from the Arctic to the Antarctic. Perversely, they blocked the way to Asia's riches. In 1507, French map makers labeled both continents *America,* after the euphonious first name of Italian Amerigo Vespucci, an explorer of the southern continent.

On the coast of the northern continent, along broad-mouthed rivers and myriad creeks, some thousands of brown-skinned hunters roamed. They knew neither the wheel nor the gun nor the metal sword. At first these nearly naked people looked with awe at the finely dressed white visitors, then fought them savagely when ships brought hundreds at a time to take over their hunting grounds.

"Cabot may have seen two natives running along the shore," archivist Elizabeth Ralph told me in Bristol, "but they were so far away he could not be sure." In the old heart of the city, we had stopped to read a memorial to Cabot. My companion pointed out *Matthew*'s docking place, a stone quay on the narrow river Frome.

"What did Cabot bring home to prove he'd found Asia?" I asked.

"Nothing—except maybe a little water. He went ashore only once. He raised the English flag to claim the land, and filled the water casks," she said.

Accounts say he found campfire ashes, snares for game, and a stick painted red with holes in both ends. Quickly Cabot left. He couldn't risk his 18 men and limited supplies in a meeting with strangers who might be hostile. Probably Cabot had no dry powder for his guns.

Cabot's lone ship was about the size of the 70-foot *Nina,* smallest of Columbus's three. I could imagine Cabot, with a heavy Italian accent, excitedly telling Bristol's sea captains, and the king in London, how he guided the *Matthew* along the same straight-line route across the featureless ocean and back home again. To stay on course, he constantly measured his latitude by the North Star, probably using an astrolabe instead of guessing as most captains did.

No one knows Cabot's exact landfall, or the harbor where he put ashore. Many historians pick Nova Scotia or Cape Breton for one or both, and when I visited Newfoundland, I found strong claims there. Occasionally someone finds a "Cabot stone," a rock supposedly bearing a message from Cabot. In the museum at St. John's, Newfoundland's capital, I saw a photograph of one taken at Grates Cove showing faint, puzzling scratches. And at Torbay, ten miles north (Continued on page 16)

Determined gaze and set of chin mark this 16th-century artist's conception of Christopher Columbus, whose voyages of discovery led to the conquest and settlement of two continents. Columbus himself drew the sketch-map below of the northwest corner of the island of Hispaniola. Exploring this coast, on December 25, 1492, Columbus lost his flagship, the Santa Maria, *when it ran aground on a sandbar. His map shows the site of the first New World settlement, Nativida, or La Navidad, established a few days after Christmas of 1492.*

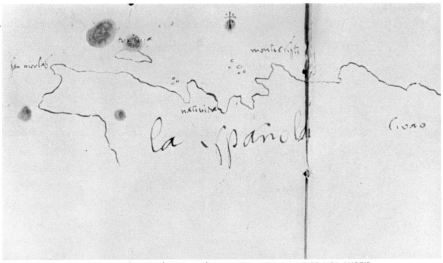

METROPOLITAN MUSEUM OF ART, NEW YORK (DETAIL, TOP); COLLECTION OF THE DUKE OF ALBA, MADRID

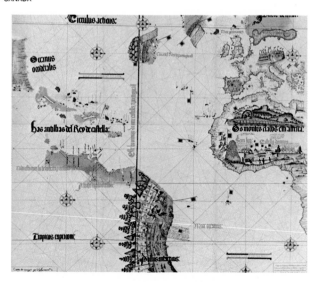

Early maps tell the story of the Old World's expanding knowledge of the New. Alberto Cantino's map of 1502 (below, left) traces the east and north coasts of South America, includes the islands of the Antilles, and—to the northwest—the tip of a land mass that scholars take as either the Yucatán or Florida peninsula. The papal line of demarcation, granting Portugal all territories to the east and Spain those to the west, runs vertically left of center. In 1506 Venetian cartographer G. M. Contarini produced the world map at left; it shows neither North nor South America. The oriental province of Tangut, arching below the polar region toward northern Europe, refers to land mentioned by Marco Polo. Contarini placed the Antilles in mid-ocean, with Zimpangu, Japan, lying between them and Cathay, China. A 1529 Spanish map drawn by Diego Ribero (below) shows greater detail and land—"tiera"—claimed by explorers, among them Portugal's Gaspar Corte Real, and Spain's Estévan Gomez, Lucas Vásquez de Ayllón, and Juan de Garay.

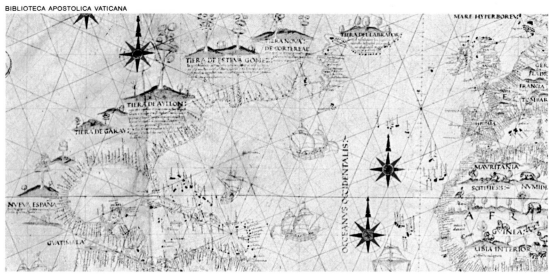

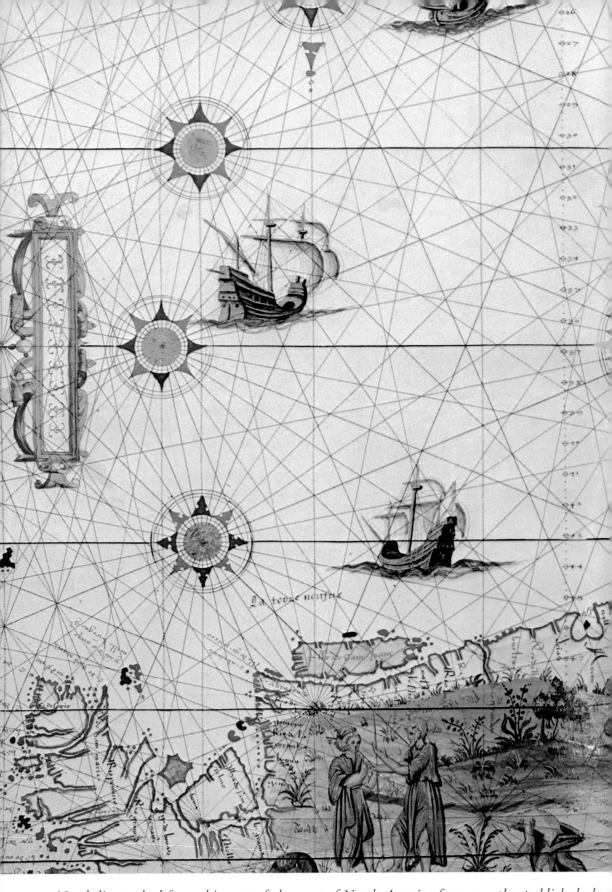

La terre neufue

North lies to the left on this map of the coast of North America from an atlas published abou[t]
1540. Florida and the Antilles appear at upper right, Newfoundland at far left. The map fo[llows]

La florida

include the results of Cartier's discoveries in the Gulf of St. Lawrence in 1534-5. The
d's interior holds robed people, fanciful plants, lions, bearlike beasts, and a unicorn.

Ships line the quay at Bristol, England, in this painting dated about 1700.
Here the port looks much as it did two centuries earlier, in 1497, when its
10,000 residents heard the news that adopted citizen John Cabot had found
land across the western ocean. Bristol merchants invested heavily in New World
explorations seeking a water route through the continent to China.

of St. John's, I heard about another Cabot stone from a white-haired fisherman
named Jack Dodd, who said he had found it.

"It were buried in Treasure Cove here," Jack told me. We had walked to a rocky
slope on Torbay harbor. Near a curve in the shore, he pointed out a tiny niche in the
rock. "Righten underneath a water chute here, I took notice one day, and rooted out
this lump of concrete," he confided, his blue eyes shining in a face seamed by work
and weather at sea. "Concrete?" I asked skeptically.

"Yes. And I put it in my packsack, brought it home, and dried it in the oven. It
cracked, and I could see a brown stone inside. So I got myself a little hammer to
knock off the spoil. I began to see some letters. The name of *Matthew,* the name of
Cabot, and June 24, 1497, that's on it. And a hat like the Pope wears. So, I'm thinking that proves Cabot came ashore at Torbay. The stone? Oh, it's lost somewheres
in my closet."

News spread quickly about Cabot's short run in the northern latitudes to the
"newfound land," and of its solid sea of fish. Powerful Spanish fleets might keep the
rest of Europe's seamen out of the gold-laced islands of the south, but nobody cared
if they took a treasure in fish from the northern sea. There was more than enough

for everybody in the waters above the continental shelf and the flat-topped underwater mountains stretching off Newfoundland—today's Grand Banks. Cabot's son Sebastian, who went on a second exploring trip during which his father's ship and three others were lost, described "so great multitudes of certeyne bigge fysshes . . . that they sumtymes stayed [the] shippes."

During the early 1500's, from March to September, hundreds of fishermen pulled up codfish on their lines and sliced, salted, and barreled tons of fillets on the decks of their smelly, bouncing vessels. At first the fishermen sailed to Newfoundland's bays and harbors only to take on water and wood before turning home. But about 1520 the English in particular based themselves on land, living in wooden houses while they dried codfish fillets in the New World sun.

By that time, Spanish soldiers, in debt and bored with sugar and cattle plantations on warm Caribbean islands and the small profits taken from slave-worked gold mines, had gone to Mexico. News of galleons hauling Aztec gold to Spain suddenly endowed all the New World—still a misshapen strip of land on some maps—with a shimmer of gold. Explorers began to map the Atlantic coast, and for a century of gold madness, Spanish, French, and English prospector-settlers attacked the northern mainland with shovels and pickaxes and wild expectations.

I read firsthand accounts of their incredible blunders, hardships, and failures. They all began with flags flying and cannons booming as a great crowd of people, domestic animals, and goods boarded cumbersome ships bound for vague New World areas with mysterious names like Florida, Chicora, Canada. I filled a chapter with the amazing tales of those who lived through months or years of violence and tragedy in remote, wild—and goldless—lands.

People and villages began to survive when their purpose became permanence and work, when leaders had practical minds, inexhaustible energies, and brutal tenacity, and when food arrived from the outside world while settlers spent a year or two learning the climate and the soil.

Spanish St. Augustine, guardian of the treasure route along the Gulf Stream off Florida's east coast, was the first settlement north of Mexico to survive the mainland's terrors. Pedro Menéndez, vigorous, audacious, and a merciless slaughterer of his enemies, forced it into life. Supplies from nearby Havana, Cuba, kept it going. In contrast, stranded English farmers 500 miles north on Roanoke Island were engulfed by the wilderness—the famed "Lost Colony."

While journeying along the East and Gulf coasts from Newfoundland to New Orleans, I lingered over "firsts"—the first landing, the first street in the first village, the first leaders. Fortunately the first leaders of the first four settlements north of Florida wrote detailed and stirring accounts—John Smith at Jamestown, Samuel de Champlain at Port Royal and Quebec, and William Bradford at Plymouth.

Their colonies became food-producing bases, assuring later arrivals that they would have no "starving time" in the new country. For Puritans at Boston, Catholics in Maryland, Scandinavians in Delaware, Quakers in Pennsylvania, food was only a few hours or a few days away. And the old-timers' experience with Indians and woodland life provided quick schooling in vital skills. Like one Dutchman at New Amsterdam, new arrivals could say after a few weeks, "I was wilderness wise. I could handle a gun or an axe, manage a canoe, (Continued on page 24)

In a summer sunset, Newfoundland waters gleam like a field of marigolds as a fisherman sculls his dory homeward. Such fine days, especially if the catches come in big and plentiful, have made life worthwhile for hardworking Newfoundlanders since the early days of the cod fishery on the Grand Banks in the 16th century. Generations of fishermen have followed the cod, which first appear on the banks from deeper waters in March and stay as late as September to spawn. In the months ahead, the islanders face long, cold winters, when frozen fog tats the siding of old buildings with crystalline lace.

Men and women from Portugal and the Azores settle a nameless colony at the edge of a Cape Breton harbor about 1522. There, led by João Alvares Fagundes, they hoped to farm and fish

stead of salting their catches and shipping them back home, fishermen could dry them on the
un-warmed sands. The duration, the fate, and even the location of the colony remain in doubt.

Pale northern sun, enfeebled by low-hanging clouds, highlights a canoeist paddling acro

SAM ABELL

lewfoundland fjord. The cold, deep waters of these craggy inlets reach as far as 90 miles inland.

speak a few guttural Indian words, and fall silent when silence was necessary."

Near the Delaware River in Pennsylvania where Finns lived deep in the woods, I searched out a log cabin built in 1642, one of the first in America. In its shadow I contemplated the danger, the isolation, and the problem of finding food every day of the year. Among the tall trees of that quiet place, I recalled that such life-and-death realities determined the settlers' evaluations of each other—with a canny hunter and fighter placing well ahead of an educated, desk-bound gentleman. Ownership of fifty or a hundred acres of land also dramatically changed settlers' views of themselves. Class-restricted Europeans swiftly shed their humble demeanor—an alarming development, some of the more aristocratic settlers thought. "When they get here," complained Swiss Baron Christopher de Graffenried on Carolina's coast, "[they] immediately become puffed up and want to be masters themselves."

Second-generation Americans moving away from the first villages into virgin areas felt so puffed up and self-confident that they began at once practicing with small revolutions for the big one to come in 1776. During a rowdy year beginning in 1700, New Jersey Puritans overturned furniture in the courthouse, snatched off judges' wigs, and locked up their absentee proprietors' governor and sheriff. Earlier, in the Albemarle Sound area, transplanted Virginians "shut one of their proprietors' governors in a chicken coop," my friend Capt. Nat Fulford told me at Hertford, North Carolina. And in Charles Town, an English outpost deep in the south, militia long accustomed to fighting Georgia Indians, Florida Spanish, and Gulf Coast French, drew up their loaded cannons in 1720 and drove their proprietors' governor away.

About the time the Americans, grown nearly three million strong, began their war in 1776 against King George III, who had bought out all the proprietors, the settlement stories of the continent's west coast began. Over plains, deserts, and mountains I flew a distance equal to Cabot's route from Bristol to Newfoundland. On the Pacific coast I found that although the Spanish and Russian settlement stories took place two or three thousand miles apart they were closely intertwined. Strong leaders, Father Junípero Serra in California and Russian fur trader Aleksandr Baranov in Alaska, charged them with color and drama.

John Cabot, of course, couldn't have imagined that such a place as Alaska existed on the far western edge of his newfound land. And Columbus insisted until his death that all the land he had explored on four journeys was Asia.

But the isles that each discovered, palm-fringed in the Caribbean or along the iceberg routes of the Labrador Sea, served as bases, take-off points for the mainland. From the islands, explorers set out for the Atlantic coast, probing and mapping Florida, the Outer Banks and the inland sounds to the north, the great bays and harbors beyond that, Cape Cod, the gulf that rimmed Newfoundland on the west. Then from those same island springboards, settlers bound for the mainland took on their last supplies. To those remaining behind they waved their last goodbyes as sails billowed and moved them toward an uncertain fate on the mainland shores.

Samuel de Champlain used this mariner's astrolabe during his exploration of the Ottawa River in the spring of 1613, some historians believe. The brass-plated instrument, five inches in diameter, enabled navigators to determine their latitude through observation of the position of the sun or of the North Star.

JUAN PONCE de LEÓN

Island Triumphs, Mainland Defeats
1492 ★ 1561

"Ponce de León, Balboa, Cortés, Coronado, all the famous conquistadors lived in these soldiers' quarters," restoration architect Manuel Del Monte told me in Santo Domingo. We were walking through newly repaired arches and onto secluded patios of a dozen or so coral-block row houses. "They were built after a hurricane in 1502 leveled wooden houses put up a few years earlier on the opposite side of the river."

From the row houses we strolled across the parade ground toward the arcade of Viceroy Diego Columbus's palace. Over the tops of palm and banana trees, I saw four masts of a great sailing ship at anchor in the mouth of the Ozama River. "For historical atmosphere?" I asked. Manuel Del Monte smiled. "No, a three-day visit of Christopher Columbus. Would you like to meet him?"

And so I went to a ceremony at Diego's palace honoring Christopher the 18th, an officer-cadet making a world cruise on the Spanish navy's training ship. "In every generation since Diego, there's been a Christopher Columbus," he told me. "And I have always wanted to come here. I feel very much at home."

Christopher's famous ancestor began his first American settlement at La Navidad,

Discoverer of Florida and, tradition says, seeker of the fountain of youth, Juan Ponce de León set foot on the peninsula in 1512, naming it for Easter Sunday — Pascua Florida. Returning nine years later to establish a colony on the west coast, he met with hostile Caloosa Indians, who wounded him mortally.

16TH-CENTURY SPANISH HELMET (ABOVE)

Restored palace of Columbus's son Diego stands in Santo Domingo, first permanent European settlement in the New World, built on Hispaniola in the 1490's. Of the Caribbean, Columbus wrote that it "is a place to behold and never leave."

on the northwest coast of Hispaniola. There, soon after Christmas, 1492, Columbus left about 40 volunteers to build and man a fort, then sailed for Spain to tell of his discovery and to recruit more colonists. In 1493 he returned with 17 ships carrying 1,200 men — sailors, soldiers, artisans. He found La Navidad burned, his men gone.

Columbus chose another spot, on the northeast coast, to begin again. His colonists unloaded weapons, tools, livestock, seeds, and sugarcane roots. They put up some 200 stick-and-thatch huts and called their new village Isabela. Most of them expected to grow rich without much effort and go home in a few years to spend their gold. Five years later, the colony moved south to Santo Domingo, where the harbor was better and the breezes gentler. By that time the Spanish had established a pattern they would repeat in the New World for two centuries: Columns of gentlemen-soldiers would ride horseback through forests and over mountains, looking for gold and for Indians to rob, to torture for tribute, and to enslave on plantations. At the time a Spanish fleet of 30 ships arrived in 1502 with 2,500 new settlers, most of the 300,000

Indians of Hispaniola were dead, many from smallpox, and slaves had been imported from Africa to work the sugarcane fields.

Ships slipped out to nearby islands to kidnap more Indian slaves. Those untouched islands excited new dreams of riches in soldier-farmers whose trifling incomes had not fulfilled their old dreams. But the Columbus family held claim to the islands, and settlers were limited to Hispaniola.

In 1508, with Christopher Columbus dead two years, Juan Ponce de León gained the viceroy's permission to try conquering one of the islands for himself. If he could subdue the Carib cannibals on the island to the east of Hispaniola, present-day Puerto Rico, he could become its governor and have all but the king's fifth of whatever gold he found. In one year, he had killed scores of Indians, started a town near today's San Juan, and built a fine house for his wife and daughters.

But suddenly his position was snatched away. Diego Columbus, the new viceroy in Santo Domingo, took Ponce's governorship and gave it to somebody else.

By then, in 1512, other soldier-farmers had been sent by Diego to take over Jamaica and Cuba. Even Vasco Nuñez de Balboa, a runaway from his debts in Santo Domingo, governed a town, Darién, in Panama.

His island lost, Ponce was granted a chance at another, Bimini, by King Ferdinand. Legend says the tough old soldier really went looking for a fountain of youth. I checked the story in accounts of the time.

Peter Martyr, secretary to the king, mentioned Ponce's search for Bimini in his *De Orbe Novo,* "Of the New World." But he said nothing about magic water. Years later, Martyr mentioned a legend that an island "named Boiuca or Agnaneo," not Bimini, had a spring whose waters "maketh owld men younge ageyne." The connection of Ponce with the fountain of youth was made by Gonzalo de Oviedo in his *Historia General y Natural de las Indias,* published 14 years after Ponce died.

While searching north of Cuba, Ponce found what he thought was a big island. On April 2, 1512, *Pascua Florida* — Flowering Easter Sunday — he smelled sweet breezes off a flat coast lined with palms and live oaks and named the land Florida. Everywhere Ponce sailed, south around Florida's tip and north up the west coast, armed Indians gathered. On at least one occasion they attacked a shore party. With his small number of men, Ponce backed off, taking no slaves and no gold, only a few casks of quite ordinary water. His most valuable find was a powerful northward-flowing current charted by his pilot along Florida's east coast — the Gulf Stream.

Ponce's "island," what he had seen of it, seemed so big that he doubted it was Bimini. He returned to Puerto Rico, leaving the crew of his companion ship to continue the search. Surely Ponce, 52 at the time, would have gone on had he thought for a moment that a fountain of youth existed.

Florida settlement waited for a decade while Ponce did the king's business — killing Indians on Carib islands — and saved money to establish the colony that would give him the title "Governor of Florida." A year or so after Ponce found Florida, news came that Balboa had cut through a hundred miles of jungle west of Darién and waded into the long-sought South Sea. Five or six years later, explorers along a coast to the west of Cuba had collected enough Indian stories of a rich inland city to excite Cuba's governor to find it.

Too busy to go himself, he sent Hernán Cortés in early 1519 with 550 men and 16

horses. Within 18 months, Cortés had conquered Montezuma's Aztec capital in Mexico, and was sending a treasure in gold and silver to Veracruz, his coastal fort.

In San Juan, Ponce, white-haired and 61, had decided he was ready to settle Florida. He began selling his property to buy ships and supplies. In February 1521, he set sail in two ships carrying 200 hired men, monks and priests, horses and cattle.

Ponce remembered the place where nine years before Indians had told him he could find gold. He went there — possibly Charlotte Harbor on the west coast. In March's unexpected chill, his men shivered in light clothing as they set up camp. "Although [the priests] preached much to them, [the Caloosa Indians] were little disposed to hearken," one account says. In late July when Ponce tried to advance inland, a barrage of arrows tore into him and his men.

One ship took Ponce to Cuba. There, in the village of Havana, he died of his wounds. The other ship crossed the great gulf south to Veracruz. Cortés's soldiers, besieging rebellious Aztecs in Mexico City and short of gunpowder, cheered the timely arrival of Ponce's forces.

News of the successes of Cortés arrived in Spain as Judge Lucas Vásquez de Ayllón of Santo Domingo visited the court of Charles V. He asked permission to start a settlement north of Ponce's Florida on a coast called Chicora. Perhaps that land might hold riches such as Cortés had found. Ayllón's guileful Indian captive, Francisco, told the king a fantasy of glories — giant kings, pygmy people with tails like crocodiles, and, of course, a wealth of pearls and gold.

"We sent [Ayllón] back to New Spain," wrote Peter Martyr, "authorizing him to build a fleet to carry him to those lands. . . . Companions will not fail to join him. They are ready to sacrifice what they have for what they hope they can get."

Four years passed before Ayllón could finish his duties as judge and convert his fortune into ships and supplies. In mid-July of 1526, six ships left Santo Domingo with 500 men and women — a hundred of them African slaves — goats, swine, chickens, and 90 horses. At that moment, Ayllón saw himself as the founder and governor of the first permanent settlement on the mainland north of Mexico. Everything seemed favorable — a site scouted by explorers, an Indian interpreter, optimistic colonists, supplies only a few weeks away in Cuba.

Three months later, at least half the settlers were dead, their village was ruined by fire, and the survivors were crowding onto ships for home.

On marshy land by a river, in muggy heat amid a plague of mosquitoes, slaves and artisans had built their settlement, San Miguel, probably in present-day South Carolina. Indians living nearby came to watch. Before long, settlers began to sicken with fever and die. Ayllón himself died October 18. Two mutineers seized control and for weeks tyrannized the settlers. The Indians began picking off people one by one.

One night the grim events reached a wild finale. Slaves set fire to a house with the mutineers inside. As both ran out, settlers grabbed swords and captured them. More

Overleaf: Spaniards abandon their colony of San Miguel, perhaps on today's Carolina coast, in the chill of winter 1526. Their commander, Lucas Vásquez de Ayllón, and 350 of their comrades lay dead. Discouraged and ill, the survivors head for Santo Domingo. Not until the founding of St. Augustine in 1565 did Spain establish a permanent settlement on the mainland north of Mexico.

houses caught fire. Before the ashes stopped smoking, one mutineer was tried and hanged, the other held prisoner, and the colonists had voted to leave at once for Santo Domingo. On the way, seven died of exposure in sudden icy weather, and fierce storms swept many into the sea. Only 150 made it home, in December of 1526.

Six months later, hundreds more started from Spain to conquer Florida. One-eyed Pánfilo de Narváez of Jamaica, who had failed in a plot in 1520 to kill Cortés and take his place as governor of Mexico, determined to outdo him in Florida.

Leaving a hundred men to build a fort at today's Tampa Bay, Narváez's column of 300 foot soldiers and cavalry headed north, swimming streams, splashing across swamps, and hacking through forests. Visions of a rich Indian city pulled them on. "Apalache" was such a place, they heard repeatedly from Indians who pointed away from their own villages. The invaders walked a thousand miles, until they reached southern Alabama, robbing and fighting angry Indians whose long, heavy bows drove arrows through their armor. At last they found Apalache (near Tallahassee) — a few dozen huts, a few bushels of corn — and Indians attacking from the woods. Narváez and his men retreated to the coast to rendezvous with his ships. None came. On a desolate beach, the men built raft-boats, and killed their horses for food.

Hugging the coast, they headed for Mexico. One day, a hurricane struck the boats. Most of the men drowned. Some were washed ashore, only to starve or be captured by Indians. Just four conquistadors lived to see Mexico — six years later. Stopping in Indian villages along the way, they had walked across Texas, New Mexico, and Arizona before reaching a Spanish outpost in Sinaloa, on the Gulf of California.

From Cabeza de Vaca and his companions, the Spanish learned the enormous width of the continent. And from them they heard stories of fabulous lands, thundering herds of humped cows, amazing cities. Cabeza wrote down his story. Hernando de Soto read it, talked to Cabeza and in 1539 quickly organized another 600 noblemen to go to Florida. For four years they sought non-existent gold over 6,000 miles of southeastern wilderness, plundering and killing Indians, losing their leader and half the men. On rafts, the 311 survivors at last floated 600 miles down the Mississippi River and around the Gulf of Mexico. And during their last two years of wandering, another band of conquistadors, led by Francisco Coronado, rode north out of Mexico and through Arizona deserts to the plains of the Kansas and Texas Indians looking vainly for Cabeza's golden cities.

As for the hundred town builders Narváez left in 1528 at Tampa Bay, they boarded ship and left after a year of waiting — except for one man De Soto found there a decade later living as a slave among the Indians. Years would pass before Spaniards again grappled with the mainland north of Mexico.

Taking leave of the Spanish, I flew one July day to Newfoundland, far to the north, where English fishermen were living half of each year in the early 1500's. From above, I saw glistening lakes slashing the dark land. A shoreline of slender, stony fingers reached miles out into the white-capped ocean. Warm winds rippled St. John's landlocked harbor on the island's Avalon Peninsula. The summer was unusually warm, much like the one Cabot experienced: no icebergs, and very little fog. Treeless slopes rose from the bay, and on the gentle heights of one side, I saw with surprise a spread of houses for more than 100,000 people.

"There's a lot more to St. John's than I imagined," I said to Frank Stevens, at the

In an April snowfall an overturned boat awaits the coming of spring on a Newfoundland beac

freezes, blows, turns sunny, . . . rains, snows," says a resident of his island's winters.

visitor center. "That's probably what English explorer John Rut thought in 1527 when he found ten fishing ships here," Frank replied. We were looking toward the city from one high shoulder of the narrows that connect ocean to harbor through the rock-wall coast. Outside, waves whipped against 600-foot-high cliffs.

Although English explorer John Cabot discovered the "newfound land," it never bore his name. For nearly a hundred years it appeared on maps as a Portuguese possession. The Bristol merchants and Henry VII concluded that Cabot had not found Asia, but that it lay somewhere beyond. While they spent money, ships, and men in futile probes for a passage through the icebergs, a Portuguese nobleman, Gaspar Corte Real, reached Newfoundland.

Corte Real explored the coast in 1500. Cartographers misplaced Newfoundland on his country's side of the line chosen by the Pope to divide the New World between the two quarreling sea powers, Spain and Portugal. For generations, Spain respected the claim, since no instruments existed to measure longitude precisely.

Yet, from Cabot's day on, Portuguese, French, English, and Spanish Basque fishing ships all worked the fog-curtained waters as far as 200 miles off Newfoundland.

Coming back year after year, the fishermen discovered that the cod swarmed close to shore in early summer—not only around Newfoundland but also nearby Cape Breton Island to the south. This knowledge led Portuguese shipowner João Alvares Fagundes to establish a fishing colony on Cape Breton about 1522. Fagundes must have heard many stories of the storms and hardships at sea. Transporting bulky barrels of brined cod and drying the fish at home must have offended his sense of profit. A fishing village would reduce the dangers and require only one ship to bring home tons of fillets dried in the New World sun.

According to Indian legend, Fagundes and as many as 200 settlers lived in a nameless village at present-day Ingonish on the island's northwestern peninsula.

On a ski lift overlooking small twin bays, I talked with a resident of Ingonish who had never heard that Portuguese had settled there 450 years ago. "Folks here live an isolated life. Fishing's good, and then there's the tourists coming in winter to ski, and in summer to swim," she said. "Wonderful summers, as you see. Winter? Gray skies, snow, storms. Beautiful, miserable."

Fagundes' settlers may have lasted only two winters, when "the rigor of the season and the cold made them abandon their settlement," as Samuel de Champlain wrote a century later. Earlier French and Portuguese heard that Indians killed the colonists the first year. But the settlement may have lasted much longer, for one Francisco de Souza wrote in 1570 that he intended visiting a Portuguese settlement started on Cape Breton "45 or 50 years ago," and from which news still came. Whatever happened, or when, Fagundes' daughter recorded that her father lost all his money.

While Fagundes' colony was fading into obscurity, a French sea captain scouting and fishing off Newfoundland's northern tip learned of a strait there. Newfoundland was an island! What lay beyond it to the west? The elusive passage to China? Perhaps he, Jacques Cartier, could find what so many others sought. Back home, his king, Francis I, needed little persuasion to pay for a voyage.

On his first journey, in 1534, Cartier explored the great gulf west of Newfoundland. From a hunting party of Indians at one of his many landings, he took on board two sons of Huron Chief Donnaconna, who trusted Cartier to bring them back in a year. They spoke of their distant town as Stadacona, today's Quebec, and their land as Canada, which seemed to mean "our place." Its great river, the St. Lawrence, they called Hochelaga.

Next year, Cartier, with 112 men in three ships, did bring home the two Hurons, now able to speak French. At the huge mouth of the Hochelaga, his fleet rested on the feast day of Saint Lawrence. Inland 500 miles, the ships reached Stadacona. Its wood-and-bark houses sprawled on a narrow ledge at the base of a 300-foot-high rock promontory. There a smaller stream flowed into the Hochelaga. Beyond the junction the river narrowed and bore the Indian name Quebec.

From an excursion boat, I gazed at the sight described by Cartier. Just past rock palisades and forested Isle d'Orléans, the rock of Quebec faces a three-mile-wide section of the river. What a moment it must have been when Cartier's ships anchored by the village—ecstatic crowds of nearly naked Indians singing at the tops of their voices, women dancing in water up to their knees. On shore, they swarmed around the white men, kissing their arms in greetings.

Soon Cartier, determined to find the China Sea, left with a crew in longboats. Upriver 150 miles, they reached a town named Hochelaga, where Montreal stands today. On a momentous October day, Cartier and 28 men armed only with pikes and trumpets carried off with remarkable poise a visit with the chief and a thousand admiring Indians. He laid hands on the sick, read from the Bible; his men sounded trumpets, enrapturing the Indians. But a few hours later, Cartier saw from the summit of a nearby mountain he named Mont Royal that rapids blocked the route to China.

Through the long winter, Cartier and his men lived in a fort near Stadacona, enduring shoulder-deep snow—and cold so intense that ice in the river froze 12 feet thick. A deadly ailment attacked the men. "Some lost all their strength...sinews contracted...teeth all fell out"—the symptoms of scurvy. Men died painfully until one of the French-speaking Hurons told Cartier about a curing tea brewed from a certain evergreen. Ships and men followed the breaking ice of spring to the Atlantic, taking Donnaconna and nine relatives, kidnaped in a moment of pique.

The Hurons, taken to France, never returned, but Cartier did, after five years. King Francis I decided that Donnaconna's gold-laced tales about a northern land called Saguenay meant Canada had more riches than China. In the spring of 1541, Cartier guided five of the king's ships packed with gentlemen, artisans, men and women recruited from jails, livestock, and poultry to Stadacona. Sieur de Roberval, appointed chief over Cartier, planned to follow soon with 200 people.

Roberval didn't show up. Cartier's 300 settlers built a fort at Cap Rouge just beyond Stadacona, searched upriver for Saguenay until stopped by the rapids, picked up barrels of sparkling rocks, and lost 35 men in an Indian attack.

As I read the accounts, I had the feeling that Cartier's first winter in Canada, in 1534-35, had left him less than eager for a second, and when it ended, no one had to talk him into pulling out before Roberval arrived.

Cartier's men stopped at St. John's—and encountered Roberval, who ordered them back to Quebec. Cartier slipped away by night for France. Roberval went on to Stadacona. His 200 gentlemen and ladies sang and danced, excited by dreams of the gold and diamonds they thought they had seen in Cartier's barrels. Actually Cartier's sparkling rocks were iron pyrites and quartz.

Cape Smoky thrusts a stony rampart from Ingonish Bay on Cape Breton Island. Portug.

tlers in the 1520's beached their boats and cured their catches on the bay's level shore.

At Cap Rouge, the settlers sobered more each month. Often hungry and sick and shut inside, they became lean, tense, and hateful through the long winter. Scurvy killed 50 — no one knew of Cartier's magic evergreen. Roberval imposed discipline with gallows, whipping post, and fetters. In spring, just before leaving, he took one quick look for Saguenay. The rapids that stopped Cartier ripped open one of the boats, and eight men drowned.

That tragedy marked the end of a half-century during which the North American mainland had worn down or grated to bits seven groups of European settlers. All — except perhaps Fagundes — lacked suitable food, clothing, timing, or intentions. Of the nearly 2,500 who came, only half survived to return home.

With nothing salable picked up from the face of the land to repay ruined investors, and with the survivors spreading horror stories, the northern mainland would excite only shudders in Europe and New Spain for 16 years.

Spain's Philip II, robbed of New World gold and silver by pirates and by hurricanes sinking his treasure fleets, decided in the late 1550's to invest once more in a permanent mainland settlement to the north. Refuge for shipwrecked Spaniards and harbor for pirate-hunting patrols, the base should be located somewhere along the route of the treasure fleets. Philip would pay a third of the cost; wealthy Spaniards in Mexico the rest. In Mexico City in December of 1558, ranch owner Don Tristan de Luna y Arellano, favorite of the viceroy and onetime conquistador with Coronado, took the oath as Governor of Florida.

From Veracruz the next June, Luna's 13 ships left the harbor with 1,500 colonists. Meticulously planned on paper, the venture could not fail. Spaniards now knew how to establish settlements, having done it 200 times in the Caribbean, Mexico, and Central and South America, where more than 100,000 Spaniards were living.

Luna had soldiers, servants, artisans, African slaves, four priests, and at least 40 men with wives and children. His ships rode deep, heavy with food and supplies. In 1559, at a landing on the Gulf of Mexico, Luna laid out around a central square a proper Spanish town where officials, courts, and notaries would set up offices.

Two years later, weeds grew in the ghost settlement of Ochuse (Pensacola), Florida, desolate memorial to its sick and financially ruined leader. Why didn't the paper plan work? Luna lost his wits, many of the men told the viceroy.

Looking at the list of disasters, I surmised that he had enough problems to drive anyone crazy: a hurricane that destroyed most of his supplies ... epidemics of fever ... a desperate 200-mile walk with a thousand people planning to live off the Indians near present-day Selma, Alabama, only to find Indians and food gone ... futile, starved rambles looking for Indians to rob of corn and to convert to Christianity ... quarrelsome, conniving officers and men. Luna spent the last six months bitterly arguing with them over what to do about their terrible situation. March back to the coast? They did. Obey Luna and march north again? They refused.

Jacques Cartier and a crew of oarsmen strain against white water in the St. Lawrence River in a futile search in 1541 for a gold-laced northern land called Saguenay. Stopped by rapids "and great rockes," he turned back. Cartier also felt the rough water blocked the route to the China Sea. A century later, Robert Cavelier de La Salle ironically named the rapids "La Chine," or China.

At least they didn't kill each other, although Luna once ordered every man hanged, then relented. On Palm Sunday 1561, a priest confronted Luna, dramatically interrupting the giving of the Sacrament. "If you believe [what] every faithful Christian must believe," he said, "how is it that you are the cause of so many evils and sins ... because you will not reconcile yourself with your captains to treat of a remedy for all this people, who for your sake have perished or are perishing ... ?"

Luna burst into tears and asked everybody to forgive him. His officers fell at his feet crying. All weeping together, they made up. Still, two days of talking produced no plan. Just then a long-awaited supply ship arrived, deciding the issue for them. They would board it and leave.

Philip II, who had lost a fortune, announced that Spain would try no more to colonize north of Mexico. If Spaniards could not get a base going on the hellish northern mainland, the French and English could never do it either. Three years later, daring Frenchmen would shock him into changing his mind.

The flyer.

Bloody Florida, Lost Roanoke 1562★1590

$\mathcal{H}$eels clack, skirts swirl, Gypsy guitars and tambourines race wildly. Shouts of *"Olé!"* heighten the revelry at the Madrid court of 1565. Suddenly trumpets blare and drums roll. "Don Philip the Second, by the Grace of God!" announces a chamberlain. Slender, blond-bearded Philip, 38, enters and greets his courtiers. Moments later, his ambassador to Paris arrives with news of disaster: "France has secretly seized our Florida territory and already planted a colony there!"

"Burn them! Kill them!" cry the courtiers.

Who should head an expedition to destroy the French settlers? Philip declares he has chosen the man. He gestures a command: Bring Pedro Menéndez de Avilés!

Soon a graying man with determined set of jaw strides in and kneels before his king. Scourge of pirates, convoy captain during years of war with France, Captain-General of New World treasure fleets, Menéndez savors the new commission.

In an audience of 2,000 at the amphitheater in St. Augustine, Florida, I watched this scene of playwright Paul Green's *Cross and Sword*. Opened on the 400th anniversary of the continent's oldest city north of Mexico, the annual summer musical

"They have commonly conjurers or jugglers which use strange gestures. . . . and fasten a small black bird about one of their ears as a badge of their office," wrote English colonist Thomas Hariot of the Indians of North Carolina's Outer Banks. His text accompanied this 1585 drawing by settler John White.

Works of artist-colonist Jacques le Moyne present a fanciful view of life among Indian neighbors of Fort Caroline, Florida, founded by the French in 1564 near present-day Jacksonville. The engraving above shows his interpretation of how the Indians hunted crocodiles and alligators. Wrote Le Moyne: The Indians "are . . . so much annoyed [by the reptiles] that they have to keep up a regular watch against them both day and night. . . ." Farmers as well as hunters, men prepare the ground while women plant seeds — maize, beans, squash, millet. Camouflaged with animal skins, left, Indians stalk deer beside a stream. Engraved by Theodore de Bry in the romantic style of the time, Le Moyne's drawings contain many inaccuracies, yet provide firsthand impressions of America through the eyes of an early settler.

In the name of the King of France, René de Laudonnière, leader of the Huguenot colony of Fort Caroline, offers alliance and friendship to King Saturiba, chief of 30 Indian villages. Here Saturiba sits beneath a bower of palms, laurels, and other aromatic trees. To his right sits his soothsayer; to his left, his councilor. Eighty of Saturiba's men helped construct the fort in July 1564.

vividly evokes what it must have been like to be a first settler with strange, sometimes terrifying, Indian neighbors, and with a dynamic leader like Pedro Menéndez.

As devoted to his Catholic religion as to his king, Menéndez felt a compulsion to sweep Florida free of the invaders. Not only were the French led by a pirate, Jean Ribault, they were Huguenots—Protestant infidels. Settling on Spanish lands along the treasure fleet's Gulf Stream route, the heretics would corrupt the Indians while French corsairs attacked galleons loaded with gold and silver.

Corsair Jean Ribault, known by his great beard, had indeed led the first of two Huguenot ventures. In 1562, he set out with five ships to explore Florida's coast. Catherine de' Medici, regent for her young son Charles IX, agreed to the expedition when told how useful a Florida colony would be as a pirate base.

Ribault chose a creek site near present-day Parris Island, South Carolina, 18 miles up Port Royal Sound. He left two dozen volunteers to complete Charlesfort, a bulwark named for his king, and promised to return soon with colonists.

But a burst of civil war in France between Huguenots and Catholics lengthened "soon" into a year. The men at Charlesfort used up everything—food, patience, and friendliness in dealing with the Indians and with each other. In desperation the survivors built a makeshift boat caulked with moss, and put out to sea. Weeks later when an English ship rescued them, they had eaten shoes, leather straps, animal skins, and at least one of their number.

Finally, with the civil war quieted, and with the secret backing of Queen Mother Catherine, the Huguenots sent three ships to Florida carrying 150 soldiers—along with artisans, servants, and four women. Leader René de Laudonnière, in June 1564, bypassed Charlesfort for a site he preferred 150 miles farther south. Five miles up a river now called the Saint Johns in Florida, the colonists started a new fort, also to take its name, Caroline, from that of young Charles.

I found a symbolic Fort Caroline a few miles east of Jacksonville. The river long ago had swallowed the hillock where the original French fort stood. One mile east, a single high point breaks the flatness; on that 100-foot bluff the colonists kept a lookout for Spanish ships.

One settler, artist Jacques le Moyne, later recorded in drawings and stories his 15 months in Florida. He was startled one day shortly after the newcomers began digging a moat to see more than a hundred Indian warriors striding toward them. Wearing feather ornaments, shell necklaces, fish-teeth bracelets, pearls, and metal pendants, the dark-skinned men stopped and quickly built a bower of palm fronds. Later, King Saturiba, youthful chief of 30 neighboring villages, walked in with an escort of 800 "handsome, strong...fellows...all under arms as if on a military expedition." The king squatted under the bower to watch what the white men did.

Through an officer who knew a few words of the Timucua Indians, Laudonnière convinced Saturiba that the French would take up arms against all his enemies. Pleased with the prospect, Saturiba left 80 men to help build Fort Caroline.

Soon, both inside and outside the fort, soldiers and workers were living in board houses with palmetto thatch roofs. Artisans built a flour mill, a brick kiln-bakery, a storehouse, and a blacksmith shop. Tailors, shoemakers, gunpowder and crossbow makers, brewers, and an apothecary went to work.

But no one among them bothered to grow food. Why should they, they reasoned, with supplies filling the storehouse, more on the way, and corn and beans growing in Indian gardens?

For a few weeks, half-a-dozen noble youths prospected for gold and silver. Disappointed, bored, homesick like the others, they too killed time smoking Indian tobacco, playing cards, making wine from wild grapes, and dancing and singing.

Curious Indians flocked to watch them. Maidens were allowed by their families to live with French settlers. Most of the eight or ten babies born the next year had Indian mothers. Hoping to save the Indians' souls, the lay minister taught hundreds of children and a few of their elders to sing French Protestant songs.

In just three months the settlers had become so discouraged and angry that some rebelled. They accused Laudonnière of lying to them, luring them with promises of gold to this miserable, isolated place. Now with ominous talk of merely surviving, he even told them what they could eat or drink.

With poison and exploding gunpowder they tried to kill him, but failed. One September night, 13 rebels stole a ship, sailed to Cuba, and took a Spanish vessel heavy with treasure. In December, 66 more settlers mutinied, chained and beat Laudonnière, then ran away in two newly built ships to become pirates.

By March 1565, the Spaniards had caught and hanged half the raiders. King Philip called on Pedro Menéndez to strike Fort Caroline mercilessly.

In a matter of weeks, 46-year-old Menéndez was wrestling with storms on the ocean route to Florida. He had heard that Ribault was starting from France with men and supplies for Fort Caroline. Not waiting in Puerto Rico for all his ships, Menéndez set off for Florida in five, trying to beat Ribault. The ships carried 700 soldiers and sailors, several priests, perhaps a few Negro slaves, and 100 "useless people" as Menéndez called farmers, artisans, officials, and their wives and children. He gambled on a dangerous shortcut through the Bahamas and, after a terrifying but fast sail of 13 days, sighted Florida on August 28, feast day of Saint Augustine. Menéndez soon discovered a fine harbor, which he named for the Saint. Not taking time to unload, he pushed north, looking for the French.

He found them some 40 miles up the coast—but Ribault had already arrived. Four big French ships lay at anchor outside the sandbars at the mouth of the Saint Johns River. Menéndez deduced that, empty of men and most of their cannons, the French ships might be captured quickly by bold action. With no enemy vessels to hinder attacks on Fort Caroline, it would fall easily.

Menéndez's captains disagreed. Impatiently, he ordered them to attack. At midnight his ships slipped through the darkness until their prows extended like dueling pikes among the prows of the French. Suddenly, a burst of Spanish trumpets. Menéndez called politely: "Messieurs, who are you and why are you here?"

A French voice passed the question back. Menéndez shouted, "My name is Pedro Menéndez de Avilés! This is the armada of the King of Spain.... In the morning I will board your ships!" Outnumbered, outmaneuvered, the French cut their anchor cables and ran, ignoring gunfire. All night the Spanish pursued—but lost them.

Now in danger of attack himself, Menéndez hurried back to St. Augustine. For five days, his men hustled ashore supplies and people. Trumpets and artillery sounding, Menéndez came ashore and knelt in the sand to hear Mass. He wrote the king describing how his men built earthworks around a communal longhouse given them by Indian villagers, "digging a ditch with their fingernails" for lack of tools.

Fort Caroline's alarmed French spent the same days reloading their ships. They lost critical time in a calm, but at last a breeze pushed them south to the attack.

Southbound on the shoreline highway I drove to St. Augustine and located historian Luis Arana. He took me about a mile north of the town's waterside plaza to a cedar- and oak-shaded park, Mission Nombre de Dios. "The original site, we think. Settlers' descriptions of creek and beach indicate the Indian longhouse sat here," he said. "But the old harbor entrance was some miles south, and even the sloops of the big ships needed high tide to ride over the shallow water covering the bar." Ribault arrived there at low tide and lost his chance to destroy the Spanish colony.

He had come within a hairsbreadth of capturing Menéndez himself and 150 men trapped in small boats outside the harbor. While the French inched closer, calling for surrender, the Spaniards strained, cursed, and prayed until they heaved their sloops over the bar and into the harbor. Ribault chose not to wait for high tide; instead he turned to chase two galleons Menéndez had just dispatched to Santo Domingo.

"Then one of September's sudden storms blew in from the north. Ribault's ships found themselves out of control, flying south," Arana said. At St. Augustine, when the storm struck, Menéndez was at Mass. Probably before the service ended, he devised a daring plan to go at once and capture weakened Fort Caroline.

Menéndez ordered a march by 500 men through drenching rain, across a flooded wilderness. His officers growled objections, but Menéndez soon was slogging along with his officers and men—200 with pikes and 300 with heavy arquebuses.

Four days later, led in rainy darkness by a French prisoner at the end of a rope held by Menéndez, they lost their way. He sent back an order for his men to halt. They waited, knee-deep in water, until in the faint dawn the prisoner saw where he was—less than a mile from the fort. The scouts closed in on a French sentry and stabbed him. As the sentry screamed, Menéndez ordered the charge.

Inside the fort a watchman curious about the commotion unbarred the gate to look out—just in time for the Spaniards to rush through. Trumpets sounded. Into the chill rain, sleepy settlers stumbled out, naked, or in nightshirts. Rapidly the Spaniards thrust pike and sword through 132 of them. Menéndez spared only 60—musicians, women, and children. Fifty men, including the artist Le Moyne, escaped. At the river's mouth, the crew of a small French ship pulled aboard Le Moyne and 25 other wretched escapees before turning for home.

Among the refugees was Laudonnière, ill and in shock. The colony he had headed for 15 months had died in one hour on September 20, 1565, and now bore a Spanish name, San Mateo. He had endured mutinies, quarrels, dire hunger, and sniping by increasingly hostile Indians. He had worked through the summer preparing a ship to sail home and stocked it with supplies bought from English privateer John Hawkins, a generous visitor. All the settlers were packed to leave when Ribault, six months late, arrived with 500 colonists, including 50 women. But Ribault had then hastened away to attack St. Augustine. In his absence Menéndez had taken Fort Caroline. What could have happened to Ribault's ships with his force of soldiers and sailors?

At the moment Laudonnière was asking that question, Ribault and his men were walking from Cape Canaveral toward St. Augustine, a hundred miles north, and toward Fort Caroline beyond. His ships had been wrecked in the sudden storm that caught them when they began pursuing the two Spanish galleons.

"This is as far as the French sailors and soldiers walked," said Luis Arana when we arrived at the beach named Matanzas—Spanish for "slaughter." We had driven 15 miles south, to an inlet at the tip of Anastasia Island. That sandbar, only a river's width from the mainland, begins at St. Augustine and ends where a quarter-mile gap of turbulent ocean and river water separates it from the next sandbar-island. "It was the tip of that next island that the shipwrecked French reached, in two groups," Arana said. "The gap of water is rough. Only a superb swimmer might get across. While the French tried to build a raft, Indians ran to St. Augustine and, on September 28, told Menéndez about a group of 200 Frenchmen. Twelve days later, they told him of a second group of 300." Both times, Menéndez led a party of soldiers to the dunes at the end of Anastasia Island, and both times he tricked the French.

Like one of Menéndez's soldiers, I waded through the slithery sands and looked down from a dune at the beach on the tip of Anastasia. There on the morning of October 11, Menéndez and two captains, dressed in French naval uniforms, strolled

back and forth as they had done to lure the first group. Soon a Frenchman swam the gap. Menéndez sent him back in a boat to bring an officer, then Ribault himself. Fruit preserves and wine were served them.

Both were taken back of the dunes; both saw the bodies of scores of slain comrades. From captives they heard of Fort Caroline's end. Ribault offered ransom, and requested ships to leave Florida. To him, Menéndez gave the same reply he had given those already lying behind the dunes: "Surrender your arms and place yourself at my mercy, that I may do with you as Our Lord may command me."

Ribault took the message back to his desperate men. Should they go on starving, fighting off Indians, or risk the mercy of the Spaniards? Half the French stole away toward Canaveral. Ribault and 150 others gave themselves up. Ten at a time they were ferried across the gap.

Then, led out of sight behind the dunes, each group listened to Menéndez: "Messieurs, I have but a few soldiers with me, and you are many.... For this reason ... you [must] march to my camp ... with your hands tied behind your backs." The men then heard an ominous question: Were there any Catholics? A few stepped forward. Menéndez spared them, along with several skilled workers and—because he liked music—the fifers and drummers.

For the others, Menéndez had drawn a fateful line, dragging his spearpoint across the sand. Secretly he ordered his soldiers: When the Frenchmen reach this line, *cut them down.* Knives, swords, and pikes sliced through 134 men. Hour after hour Ribault saw his men walk behind the dunes. And then it was his turn. By daring and treachery, Menéndez had regained Florida.

During the next two years, he worked feverishly to keep his colony alive—pawning his clothes to pay for supplies, marrying an Indian chief's sister, and scurrying along a 900-mile route to placate and feed soldiers in seven garrisons.

Menéndez also hoped to find gold. Indians pointed north toward the mountains now called the Appalachians, so he sent a prospecting party. But those few who survived Indian hostility and privation brought back no nuggets.

Like the mission-building Jesuits who came later, Menéndez tried to convert the Indians. He preached sermons and sent out soldier-missionaries. But as soon as the Christians ran out of gifts their converts usually disappeared.

Menéndez left Florida in 1567, but he went on spending his own money to support his beloved colony. Settlers and soldiers, however, loved it not at all. On two visits, in 1568 and 1571, Menéndez heard of mutinies, deaths from exhaustion, disease, or arrows, and escapes to sea or to friendly Indians whose food and women made life more bearable. By 1570, only 150 soldiers, a third of them at St. Augustine, manned the whole country. Spanish farmers, tricked by lies and promises into moving to Florida, wrote home telling how they were held against their will, "ruined, aged, weary and full of sickness." Hurricanes, Indian snipers, mosquitoes, poor sandy soil—all enlarged misery into despair. Ships had to anchor outside the harbor

Overleaf: Lost in darkness and drenched by rain, 500 Spanish soldiers from St. Augustine wait in a swamp for the order to attack French Fort Caroline. At dawn, September 20, 1565, they easily took the fort—the first Spanish victory in a two-month campaign that expelled the French from Florida.

lest the gaunt, ragged people seize a transport and flee wild shore for wild ocean.

One by one the smaller forts succumbed to Indian attacks and hunger—except for San Mateo, which died suddenly and violently in 1568. In a surprise raid, a French sea captain and his crew shot, stabbed, or hanged all 380 Spaniards at the fort and its two outposts, then leveled every building, revenge for Fort Caroline and Matanzas. Chief Saturiba and his warriors ably assisted them, hating the harsh Spaniards who insisted on a strange religion and a settled existence with only one wife to a man.

After Menéndez died in 1574, the Spanish crown took over the task of maintaining the colony. Stubbornly, Philip sent new soldiers and settlers. By 1585, St. Augustine had 300 people in a wooden fort and village, half of them soldiers.

The next year nothing remained except ashes—and frightened Spaniards hiding in the woods. Francis Drake, one of hundreds of privateers Queen Elizabeth turned loose on the Spanish, led 29 ships with 2,300 men on a grand looting tour of the West Indies. Then he swept up Florida's coast, spotted St. Augustine by its lookout tower, and closed in.

"There was abowte 250 howses in this Towne"—probably an exaggeration—"but wee left not one of them standinge," bragged one sailor. In addition, Drake's men destroyed crops and orange groves nursed to production from Spanish seedlings.

Emergency supply ships brought the village staggering back to life. Fifteen years later, newly crowned Philip III queried: Was this costly outpost worth saving? A grudging "yes" from settlers and officials continued royal subsidies for 160 years.

After Drake left St. Augustine's ashes smoldering among the palm trees, he headed directly for a long chain of sandbars off the coast 500 miles northeast. He knew that behind them the 100-man colony sponsored by Sir Walter Raleigh had lived for a year, hidden from the Spanish among the live-oak trees of Roanoke Island.

Enjoying the irony, Drake offered St. Augustine's stolen boats, furniture, pots and pans to the Roanoke men. Just as small boats finished transferring the goods from sandbar inlet to island fort and nearby village, a hurricane struck. Winds and rain and sea raged three days. While Drake fought to save his ships, the soldier-settlers of Roanoke, led by Capt. Ralph Lane, had time to ponder his offer to take them home.

Cut off for a year from families and the world, ever anxious about supply ships, increasingly nervous as Indian awe changed to anger, the colonists longed for England. They climbed aboard when Drake was ready to sail, not waiting for three men who had gone on a trip into the wilderness.

"Most of the settlers, just like Drake and Walter Raleigh, were Devon men," another Devonshire man told me in Plymouth, England. W. Best Harris, librarian and historian, sent me to see the birthplace of the colony's organizer. Down country lanes 50 miles east of Plymouth, I found a two-story farmhouse the color of Devonshire cream, its roof thatched like all the cottages in the nearby village of East Budleigh. Some miles beyond, I stopped near Torquay at Compton Castle, family home of Raleigh's half-brother, Sir Humphrey Gilbert, and home today to Walter Raleigh Gilbert, tenth-generation descendant of Sir Humphrey.

Sir Humphrey had New World colonizing fever first, I heard from Commander Gilbert, a retired Royal Navy officer. He may have caught it from Devon seamen talking about Newfoundland fish and a northwest passage through the continent to China's riches. He made one trip to Newfoundland, planning to drop off colonists in

Norumbega, now called Maine. He never reached Maine, and on the way home, a wave swamped his small open boat. Sir Walter, then about 30 years old, took up Sir Humphrey's colonizing dreams.

Warm lands near the Spanish treasure route described by Raleigh's "bold and plausible" tongue and by the skillful pen of geographer-publisher Richard Hakluyt won Queen Elizabeth. She became one of the backers helping Raleigh with the enormous cost of transporting and supplying even a small colony. But the Queen forbade Walter, a favorite like Humphrey, to risk the trip himself.

When Raleigh's first colonists had unexpectedly returned home from Roanoke with Sir Francis Drake, Sir Walter quickly sought new settlers. He persuaded 14 families to go, most of them from Devon. They and 78 single men who signed up had promise of a free trip, a year's supplies, and 500 free acres of land each.

Pedro Menéndez de Avilés, pious, yet ruthless, founded Spanish St. Augustine and ended French attempts to gain a foothold in Florida.

Perhaps the land had made them forget Captain Lane's troubles the year before with the Indians already living on those promised acres. Perhaps they believed that one of the chiefs, Manteo, returning with them after a year's visit in England, could assure their safety.

More likely the new settlers, led by John White, never expected to live near Roanoke's Indians. When they left home, the plan called for them to start a new fort in the Chesapeake Bay area, probably by the mouth of the James River, which Captain Lane had explored. But for reasons unknown to historians, their ship captain refused to take them any farther than Roanoke, where he ordered them to disembark.

Landing in small boats at a creek on the north end of the island, 117 settlers walked several minutes into the forest of oaks, loblolly pines, dogwoods, and cedars. They looked for the 15 men left by supply ships that arrived two weeks after Lane's men had gone with Drake. "We found none . . . sauing onely we found the bones of one . . ." wrote colony governor John White. He later learned from Manteo's people, whom he visited at Croatoan sandbar — present-day Hatteras — that 13 men rowed their boat away from Roanoke during an Indian attack. Perhaps they still lived, lost in the wilderness.

For White and his settlers, Fort Raleigh's earthen walls lay leveled, the storehouse within half-burned. But two-story village houses stood intact, deer browsing on vines climbing their walls. For John White it was a nostalgic homecoming to a village he had helped to build and had lived in with Lane's men the year before.

During that stay, White had time to sketch Indians, plants, and animals of Virginia, as the land was called in honor of the Virgin Queen. But his second stay ended after one month spent visiting Manteo's relatives, one of whom was mistakenly killed in a

Footprints near St. Augustine evoke the fate of 334 shipwrecked Huguenots who, with their commander Jean Ribault, fell before Spanish knives, swords, and pikes in 1565. "Surrender...that I may do with you as Our Lord may command me," Menéndez had told them. When the Frenchmen did give up, the Spaniards marched them in groups behind the dunes and slaughtered them.

raid to avenge a settler's murder. White quickly expressed his remorse, then christened Manteo as Lord of Roanoke to show his friendship.

On August 18, 1587, White's daughter Eleanor, wife of Ananias Dare, gave birth to a girl, named Virginia "because," White wrote, "this childe was the first Christian borne in Virginia." A few days later, the colonists pressured the grandfather to return with the ships to England and personally bear to Sir Walter the news that Roanoke's people must have a supply ship immediately.

John White never saw Eleanor or his granddaughter again. As I gently handled his exquisite watercolors at the British Museum in London, I shuddered at the thought of the agonizing three years he spent trying to return to Roanoke.

No ships went there, for Queen Elizabeth, to save her country from vengeful Catholic Philip of Spain, had called all English vessels to her service.

Finally, in late July 1588, coastal watchers near Plymouth sighted a great armada, its tight formation spangling the waters as far as the eye could see. At the end of two weeks, the 130 ships had been scattered in the English Channel by Elizabeth's admirals, including Sir Francis Drake. Spanish vessels, their ammunition spent, limped out the only exit — north where storms and the rocks of Ireland's coast destroyed all but 51. A vast treasure in sea power lost, Spain no longer cast its shadow on the future of North America above St. Augustine.

"While the Armada crisis absorbed England's attention, Roanoke's settlers

"We have discovered...the goodliest soile under the cope of heaven... abounding with sweete trees...." reported Ralph Lane, governor of Roanoke, the first English colony in America. At the site of the colony in North Carolina, the Thomas Hariot Trail, shaded by moss-hung trees and carpeted with berries, commemorates an early settler. Internal frictions, dwindling supplies, and fears of Indian attack led to Roanoke's abandonment in 1586. A second group of settlers, 117 in all, landed in July 1587. Three years later, they had vanished — the famed "Lost Colony."

ED COOPER

struggled with a life-or-death crisis, too," Mrs. Fred Morrison remarked when I visited Roanoke Island, North Carolina. As we walked from the waterside amphitheater past grassy ramparts outlining the original fort, Mrs. Morrison, producer of Roanoke's summertime musical drama, speculated about the settlers' fate. "Paul Green's play *The Lost Colony* suggests that the colonists—Sampson, Butler, Gramme, Dare, we know the names of all the 'lost' people—soon realized no ship would come in time to save them," Mrs. Morrison said. "So they left Roanoke.

"Possibly they floated their goods and building materials 60 miles south to Manteo's village on present-day Hatteras Island. Certainly the one word they left behind indicates that's what happened."

The word was "Croatoan," pronounced CROY-tuh-WAN by Indians. John White found it in 1590, having arranged for his own passage to America.

Arriving at Roanoke Island after dark on August 17, he and the sailors with him "espied...ye light of a great fire thorow the woods.... When we came right over against it, we...sounded with a trumpet a Call, & afterwardes many familiar English tunes of Songs, and called to them friendly; but we had no answere...."

Next morning White and his companions found the fire was "sundry rotten trees burning." Nothing remained of the colony. The houses had been "taken downe" and moved away. On a gate post of "a high palisado of great trees...in fayre Capitall letters was grauen CROATOAN, without any crosse or signe of distress...."

White's captain turned the ship toward Croatoan island, where, ironically, he had anchored for the night just before reaching the inlet for Roanoke. Weather "fouler and fouler" blew the ship away from the shore. John White watched the disappearing outline of the low Outer Banks and beseeched the Almighty "to helpe & comfort" his daughter and grandchild whom he believed still lived.

Did they? No one has indisputable evidence.

But the Lumbee Indians in present Robeson County, North Carolina, "have a strong tradition that the Roanoke colonists amalgamated with them," as historian Samuel Eliot Morison says in *The European Discovery of America*. Some blue-eyed, fair-haired types, Elizabethan words, and surnames all "bear this out," he adds. The Lumbees, he notes, earlier known as Croatoan or Hatteras Indians, migrated inland about 1650. About 1660, the Reverend Morgan Jones wandered into their midst and to his surprise "conversed in English" with them.

But did all the Hatteras clans go inland? About 1700 John Lawson, exploring North Carolina's coast, wrote that "gray-eyed" Hatteras Indians said "several of their ancestors were white people, and could talk in a Book...."

And I heard these intriguing remarks from Sheriff Frank Calhoun, 67, at Manteo on Roanoke Island: "My grandfather, born in 1830, told me that in his Indian village he lived in one of several very old two-story houses of hand-hewn timbers and boards on the mainland across from Roanoke. His blond, blue-eyed mother, Malockie Paine, we believe, was descended from colonist Henry Paine."

Saluting the corn god at harvest time, dancers present an interpretation of Indian life in North Carolina in The Lost Colony, *a symphonic drama by Paul Green. Based on the Roanoke settlers and their disappearance, the play has drawn audiences to the outdoor Waterside Theater for more than three decades.*

Settlers for a Season
1520 ★ 1608

"Why shouldn't Newfoundland's fishermen be in history books as the first permanent settlers north of Mexico?" asked Jack Dodd, fisherman, poet, and amateur historian. He challenged me one dazzling summer day as we sat in a rowboat off Torbay, half an hour's drive from St. John's, capital of Newfoundland. While our two young companions jigged for codfish, I listened to the rhythmic flow of Jack's Irish speech. Only the gulls' cries of "Kittiwake! Kittiwake!" interrupted his recitation.

"What with making use of the land for houses and storage and fish drying," Jack said, "and coming back year after year to live for months in the same place, the cod fishermen were settlers on many a bay—and they had a town at St. John's long before St. Augustine started up. That's why we call Water Street 'The Oldest Street in North America.' Local government they had too, since the 1520's. The captain of the first ship to come in were fishing admiral for the season—governor, he were.

"And a lot of men come every season. In 1564 there was a count of 50 English ships at St. John's alone—upwards of two thousand men from England, and Ireland too for sure, using the beaches to dry their fish. And off these northern coasts

Angered Indian, refused knives and tools for small skins, disarms Capt. Raleigh Gilbert. As the boat pulled away, the Indian jumped aboard, seized the match-lock musket fuse, and doused it in the water. But Englishmen and Indians parted friends after the 1607 incident at Sagadahoc in present-day Maine.

BEAVER (ABOVE) LURED EUROPEANS INTO THE WILDERNESS

there would be a regular armada—350 ships at a time, catching fish and throwing the fillets into barrels with salt for taking home, where there was plenty of sunshine for drying the cod. No less than 14,000 men in those offshore fleets, I figure. Portuguese, Spanish, and French, with many a quick-fisted Basque amongst them.

"But even though the English lorded it over the shore of St. John's and Torbay and the like, there might have been some argument over which country owned Newfoundland—England or Portugal. So in 1583, after Spain took over Portugal, Sir Humphrey Gilbert come to St. John's. Before Spain could act, he put on a little ceremony and laid the name of Queen Elizabeth and himself for sure upon the land that John Cabot had found. Then Gilbert rented out parcels of the bay shore to the fishermen, and said the renting rights could pass on to their sons.

"Newfoundland folks believe a number of fishermen then and before stayed over the winter here. It's not written, no. Fishermen didn't leave nice, neat records, but we hear how some stayed to look after things. And some had other reasons.

"Take the first settler at Torbay here. Dan McCarthy come in 1520 or thereabouts as a ship's cooper to make barrels for to put the fish in. In a fight, he hit a man so hard he thought he'd killed him. So Dan jumped overboard. He swam to shore and lived through the winter with the Beothuk Indians in their sealskin houses. Later he married an Irish girl who brought the first apple seedling to Newfoundland.

"*Settlers* I'd call men like Dan, and I'd say St. John's street and houses were a settlement. If this had happened at Jamestown, don't you know the history books would say the same as me?"

As we headed back to shore, I pondered the fact that Gilbert and all his land records were lost at sea within weeks of his St. John's ceremony, and I wondered how well Englishmen could have survived the cold winters.

I asked the question of Bert Budgell, an engineer born and brought up in Newfoundland. "Oh I'm sure they did all right," he answered. "The Norsemen survived at L'Anse aux Meadows, on the far north tip of Newfoundland—why not the English on the Avalon Peninsula, in the southeast corner? Fishing ships brought supplies without fail. From September until Christmas the weather's usually stable inside the bays—in the 40's and 50's and not much fog. From then till May, it freezes, blows, turns sunny, blows hard, rains, snows, blows some more."

He pointed out that root vegetables—carrots, potatoes, yellow turnips, beets— and hardy cabbages mature in short summers and store well through winter. "And in season the men could pick bake-apple berries, squash berries, and partridge berries for making jam. As for meat, they had fish, seals, saltwater ducks, caribou, bears tasting like young pork, and in some places swarms of the now extinct northern penguin, the auk. Better than goose, I've read."

So with plenty of food, plenty of firewood, and no Indians—the Beothuks migrated inland for the winter—fishermen might well have found Newfoundland's winters no harder than life at sea, Bert speculated.

He suggested I go down to the Lower Battery in St. John's and see the fishermen's one-story plank houses, "not much different in style probably from some of the early ones." When I arrived at the narrow waterside ledge, I found Wilfred Pretty, about 60, in a small storage shack just outside his house, one of 20 or so along the narrow street. Dried cod, hard as old shoe soles, lay stacked on the tables. Outside on the drying racks, or flakes, a boy walked among the hundreds of fish fillets, turning them over one by one. Wilf sells the fish to exporters.

Wilf told me of a storm in 1965 when the sea lifted boats, flakes, and wharf into the air—"Took them away from us." And then he swung into a litany about the creatures of the sea—the writhing squid, the mile-wide schools of fish.

"Oh, but it's the little capelin the big fish are awaiting for. Greenish-gray and six inches long, they come in waves like the ocean they're in. May and June they come, day and night, to spawn on the beaches. Even with the whales and the sharks, the flatfish and the salmon, and the cod down behind them eating and eating, the capelin pile up on shore a foot deep. With baskets we scoop them in, wonderful bait and wonderful eating."

I was for crediting the Newfoundland fishermen with the first permanent English settlement in the New World—on an island as the Spanish had done on Santo Domingo. I looked up Keith Matthews, professor of history at Memorial University in St. John's, to ask, like Jack Dodd and engineer Budgell and even like the motto on Humphrey Gilbert's coat of arms, "Why not?"

Dr. Matthews answered in the quick, blurred speech of Devonshire, his home until moving to St. John's a few years before. "Settlement?" he said. "To my mind a

Amid boisterous farewells, English ships prepare to leave the crowded harbor of Portsmouth. From this and many other European ports, colonists crossed the Atlantic to find freedom and to pursue dreams of gold, furs, and land.

Summer encampment of Micmac Indians abounds with shore birds. A nomadic tribe of the Maritime Provinces, the Micmacs built canoes of birchbark to travel Canada's lakes and rivers. In winter they stalked moose and caribou. Encountering French explorer Samuel de Champlain in 1604, they welcomed him with game birds and venison. For two centuries the Micmacs allied themselves with the French, fighting against their English and Indian enemies.

settlement is a group of people who expect to live in a new place indefinitely. At St. John's, the fishermen's crude cookhouses stayed year round, but the people didn't. Only after 1610 did the records show that settlers came to start a colony."

So in the absence of earlier records, historians call St. John's a summer fishing port, a winter ghost town, a semi-settlement—until after Jamestown.

Still this toehold deserves credit as England's "transition from the Old World to the New," as Canadian historian William S. MacNutt phrases it. For even if few Dan McCarthys had settled on these north shores when the 17th century arrived, other thousands had taken home to England each autumn for a century their New World experiences and descriptions, talking of them in taverns and over teacups. By 1607, going to the New World was a familiar idea to people of Bristol, Plymouth, and Dartmouth, as well as London—and many of them later came to America to live.

Southwest of St. John's a thousand coldwater miles along the coast, at the Port Royal National Historical Park in Nova Scotia, I found another pre-Jamestown settlement story. In 1605, beside a small basin with a narrow mouth opening into the Bay of Fundy, Samuel de Champlain oversaw the building of a fort. For about three years, he and a small group of French gentlemen, artisans, soldiers, and farmers called this "habitation" their home. They departed in the same summer of 1607 that Englishmen founded Jamestown, but new settlers—sometimes French, sometimes English—came to Port Royal through the years, were uprooted, came again.

"You might call Port Royal the first permanent off-and-on settlement north of Mexico," remarked Bob Patterson, who had retired to its rolling green land, sparkling bay, and forested low mountains. "The English considered everything north of Maine as an extension of New England. Incidentally, our climate is milder than Boston's. The French considered Acadia, as they called Nova Scotia, part of New France. So the 150-year shoot-out for possession of the continent began at Port Royal, the first lingering French settlement."

Champlain's habitation, reconstructed, stands on the original site. In the busy parking lot one summer day, I saw a visitor pointing across the basin toward the town of Annapolis Royal on the opposite bank, and heard her tell a child, "Over there, Champlain had his gardens." "And," I almost added, "a five-minute walk from this parking lot, 400 Micmac Indians had a village."

In the habitation courtyard, which is ringed by gabled, wooden row houses, I leaned against the frame of the well's bucket and pulley and read an account of Indians and fur-trading. For it was furs, not fish, that brought Champlain and his patron, Pierre Du Gua de Monts, to Canada.

English fishermen lording it over Newfoundland's best harbors shot on sight any of the few hundred Beothuks who came near. But the French made friends with the numerous Algonquian Indians along the St. Lawrence shores—where whalers and sealers rendered oil—and along Cape Breton and Acadia, where fishermen lived in summer shacks. To the singing, fun-loving French who had brass pots, tools, and brandy to trade, the Indians brought furs, particularly beaver.

Englishmen smelling of fish might brag "The Pope and ten dollars!" for all the Spanish Catholics spending that much per hundred pounds of dried codfish to eat on Fridays. But Frenchmen could sell one shipload of furs for as much money as six shiploads of fish would bring. During the 1590's, after European hat makers discovered how to clip the hair from beaver hides and mat it into felt, French fur traders became as possessive of Canada's soft riches as the Spanish were of their silver mines in Mexico.

Eager Indians, longing for metal containers, weapons, and intoxicating drink, waded in icy water to trap the beaver. But the number of furs was limited. Indians learned to play off one trader against another, bargaining, raising their prices. Their profits cut, each trader dreamed of a royal grant excluding other traders, leaving but one to take all at his own price.

Henry IV, who had won the French throne in 1589 and quieted the religious wars with the Edict of Nantes in 1598, wanted colonies on New World land before the English could establish them. But Henry wanted colonies at no cost to himself. He offered the fur monopoly to anyone who would agree to pay for a settlement.

Three nobles tried and failed. One recruited 50 convicts and left them to shift for themselves on the treeless sands of Sable Island off the southeast corner of Acadia. When a French ship chanced upon the men five years later, fewer than a dozen of them remained alive, half-starved and clad in animal skins. Another monopolist left 16 men to winter at Tadoussac at the juncture of the Saguenay and the St. Lawrence rivers, ready to meet the first fur-trading Indians in spring. Nearly all froze to death.

De Monts, a Huguenot, "carried away by zeal and longing," made his first try in 1604. He hired Champlain, a Catholic, to go with him as geographer-cartographer and general adviser. Astute and practical, Champlain was one of the few non-Spaniards who had been admitted to the West Indies and Mexico and had taken a close look at how the Spanish planted colonies. De Monts persuaded two friends, Jean de Biencourt de Poutrincourt and the distinguished mariner François Pont-Gravé, to come along too. During the next three years, each of the three men would take a turn at heading the New World colony, always with Champlain the chief assistant. "A galaxy of men of lofty character," one historian calls them.

De Monts wanted a milder climate for his settlement than Cartier had found on the St. Lawrence. After scouting the coast of present-day Nova Scotia and New Brunswick, he chose a small island — easy to defend against Indians and English — ten miles up the St. Croix River, present boundary between Maine and New Brunswick. Its latitude is about the same as that of southeastern France; he expected the same temperate climate.

"But he didn't know about hard Maine winters," Everett Quinn told me when I went to see St. Croix, now Dochet — pronounced Doe-shay — Island. Mr. Quinn and his wife, Corice, of Red Beach, Maine, lived on Dochet five years, tending a small lighthouse, now abandoned. "That river has a 28-foot tide — it's at the entrance to the Bay of Fundy. When the wind comes up, it's hard to cross to shore. Ice in spring moves down and back with the tide, and then the river's dangerous to cross. My wife came ashore only when the weather was good and the tide was right."

But Champlain and de Monts had to send men to the mainland every day or two, for the island had no water and no firewood — they had cut all the trees for houses.

National Park Ranger David Hutchings took me in a motorboat three-quarters of a mile to the island. Its rock sides jut 35 feet out of the water. When we climbed up the ridge from the sandy point, we saw wooden stakes set up by archeologists beside the numerous graves they had found. (Continued on page 72)

Sprinkling of wild flowers brightens a Newfoundland landscape framed by wind-blown spruces; children play in the buttercup-strewn corner of a field. "The wants of other kingdoms are not felt heere," said an early admirer of the island and its short, gentle summers. A colonist, describing the plentiful wildlife, wrote of "divers beasts and fowls, black foxes, deers and otters." Others found the land cold and infertile.

SAM ABELL

Bartering for tools and weapons, Algonquians bring beaver, lynx, moose, and bear skins to a French trading post at Port Royal, Canada. Colonists began a fur trade here when the

French arrived at the Bay of Fundy in 1605. To supply a growing European market for beaver hats and fur collars, Algonquians invaded and depleted the hunting grounds of neighboring tribes.

"The settlers — 79 of them — were comfortable and healthy enough as long as it was summer," Hutchings said. "But when the biting winds and snows of winter came howling down the river, and there was no fresh food to eat, many of them sickened with scurvy. These are some of the graves of the 35 who died."

When the spring of 1605 finally brought Pont-Gravé with supplies from France, de Monts and Champlain took the ship south to look for a better site. King Henry had granted de Monts all the land to present-day southern New Jersey, ignoring claims of the English who called the same area Virginia, and the claims of the Spanish to lands from Florida to Acadia.

After ranging the coast and finding the Massachusetts Indians so knavish that "they would steal even with their feet," as Champlain noted, de Monts turned his back on fine harbors like Boston and Plymouth. A place he'd named Port Royal, across the Bay of Fundy from St. Croix Island, was safer, he felt. From St. Croix, his ships ferried men and most of the disassembled buildings to the new location.

"Champlain made drawings of the fort, or habitation, they put up here," Superintendent W. A. Stewart told me at the reconstructed fort. "We positioned the circle of houses around a well the archeologists uncovered, and followed Champlain's plan right down to the pigeon loft by the gate." He showed me the kitchen full of large ovens and caldrons and skillets. "They cooked for about 50 Frenchmen and any Indians who dropped in for dinner. They had enough food the first winter, but they still lost a dozen workmen to scurvy."

Pont-Gravé and Champlain headed the colony while de Monts went home to try to save his monopoly from jealous intriguers at court. He had spent a fortune and had small returns on his furs to show for it. When he couldn't leave the next spring, in 1606, he talked Poutrincourt into returning, taking Pont-Gravé's place, and bringing replacements for the salaried workers whose terms had ended.

Among the new arrivals was a Paris lawyer and poet, Marc Lescarbot. He wrote with humor of Micmac Indian customs — and of gourmet feasts provided by Champlain's *L'Ordre de Bon Temps,* The Order of Good Cheer.

"We still have an Order of Good Cheer in Annapolis Royal," member Arch MacIntosh told me. "It was revived about 1930, and at each monthly meeting one of the members volunteers to serve the food — just the way Champlain's plan put each of the habitation's fifteen gentlemen in the role of caterer for one day. That way, Champlain made certain that fowl and game and seafood would be gathered regularly for a good diet. Dinner began with a ceremonial parade into the great hall with its enormous fireplace. The host led, wearing a chef's hat, a napkin on his shoulder, and the badge of the order around his neck. Members followed with dishes of food. Once a year we have the procession and French chef costume. About the only thing we don't have is Membertou, the redoubtable Micmac chief."

The chief wore a thin black chin beard and looked about 50 years old, Lescarbot said, but claimed to have seen Jacques Cartier 70 years before. Membertou had moved the tribe near the French "to live in security." His Micmacs greeted their friends with a "Ho, ho, ho!" described by Lescarbot as "a salutation of joy . . . almost in laughing, testifying thereby that they are glad to see [them]." Those Micmacs who could speak a little French pronounced it well, Lescarbot said, but mingled it with "much Basque," picked up from fishermen.

Membertou danced after dining with Poutrincourt one memorable evening, and made a fiery speech about how much he loved the French—a tribute to their tact and good sense as they lived day-by-day with *les sauvages*.

Still the French wanted a location with shorter winters, so Champlain, in the fall of 1606, again scouted as far south as Cape Cod. He found that the Massachusetts Indians loved them less than ever. One night five men disobeyed orders and stayed on shore to cook cakes. At dawn, the watch on ship cried, "O Lord! our men are killed, our men are killed!" Champlain and a crew jumped from bunks to boat, but arrived too late. "As our men did sing over our dead men the funeral services ... these rascals [the Indians] ... did dance and howl a-far off...," wrote Champlain. Later when low tide would keep the French ship from coming to shore, the Indians ran to the graves, "digged out and unburied [a corpse], took away his shirt, and put it on them ... and besides all this, turning their backs toward the barque, they did cast sand with their two hands betwixt their buttocks in derision, howling like wolves." It was certainly not a year to bring white settlers to Massachusetts.

Back at Port Royal, Champlain soon learned the company had to go home. De Monts had no more money. He had failed to save his monopoly, and poachers roaming the St. Lawrence had stolen all the season's furs.

On that August day in 1607 when the French drew up anchor, Membertou and his tribe watched until the ships disappeared. "It was piteous to see ... those poor people weep," wrote Lescarbot. No one could foresee that Champlain would return the next year, but to the St. Lawrence—nor that Poutrincourt, homesick for America, would bring his family to Port Royal in 1610 to spend a few years.

Both Frenchmen would have groaned in dismay if, as they passed southern Acadia on their way home, they had seen two English ships loaded with settlers skirting that coast before turning south toward their pre-selected colony site in Maine.

Within ten days these 120 men of the North Virginia Company of Plymouth were shoveling up an earthen wall, creating Fort St. George on the Sagadahoc River, now the Kennebec. At the same time, 800 miles south and a day's sail up the James River from Chesapeake Bay, settlers of their brother company, the South Virginia Company of London, were hurrying to complete a stockade around the tents and lean-tos they had just built at Jamestown.

From a small plane I had my first view of the rocky Maine coast where the Sagadahoc colony, nearly identical to Jamestown in size and plans, tried its luck and found it all bad. A snowstorm two days before had whitened the lake-punctured forests and farms of southern Maine. Lumpy islands by the dozen littered a coastline indented with small bays, coves, and river mouths. Pilot Howard C. West pointed out the Kennebec, wide and ice-free as it opened into the Atlantic. "But I've seen it frozen all the way to the ocean when it's really cold."

At Augusta, 50 miles north upriver, the Kennebec lay frozen solid, edged with dark pines, spruces, cedars, and leafless oaks, maples, and birches.

In the Maine State Archives and Museum, Sylvia Sherman showed me a copy of a picture map of Fort St. George "drawn in 1607 by a settler and found 280 years later in the Spanish archives. Who knows how it got there?" she said. Spaniards kept a hostile watch on English settlements in America despite a 1604 peace treaty. But they left the colonists alone, hoping they would die or run away.

WALTER MEAYERS EDWARDS (ABOVE); INFORMATION CANADA-PHOTOTEQUE

Winter ice blocks Canada's "front door" at Cape Breton Island. Vikings first visited the Canadian coast about A.D. 1000. In the early 1500's, hardy Bretons established a fishing station and gave the island its name. Fishermen from Portugal, Spain, and England also plied these waters, coming to shore for wood and water. Frenchmen frequented St. Ann's Bay; the present Sydney Harbor bore the name of Baye des Espagnols; and today's Louisbourg—an 18th-century French fortress (above and left)—rose on the site of Port aux Anglais. In the 16th century, Frenchmen and Englishmen began quarreling over Cape Breton harbors, prelude to their long struggle for the continent.

England's James I provided no money to support the two Virginia settlements, for 20 years of war with Spain had emptied his treasury. Only merchants had surplus money for expensive and risky investments.

Merchants were prospering from the boom in peacetime trade. In the late years of Elizabeth's reign, they had organized themselves into companies—the East India, the Levant, the Merchant Adventurers, the Muscovy Company—pooled their capital, occasionally selling stock to investors, and financed large ventures in Asia and Africa. Now with unspent profits and much experience starting trading posts, they pondered enticing reports from explorers about their king's lands in America. But it took a few excited landowners and wealthy men of the professions to draw merchant capital into American colonizing ventures.

Five Indians kidnaped from Maine's coast by Capt. George Waymouth in the summer of 1605 triggered the action. Waymouth captured them for a Catholic group wanting firsthand information from American natives about a colony site, a refuge from increasing persecution. But when Waymouth returned to England, Plymouth's fort commander, Sir Ferdinando Gorges—no friend of Catholics but an old admirer of Walter Raleigh and his colonizing dreams—kept the Indians for himself.

Three of them lived in his home in the little Devon port, and as they rapidly learned English from a tutor, Gorges questioned them about their homeland. He became more and more excited by their descriptions of "goodly rivers, stately islands, and safe harbors."

Quickly, 40-year-old Gorges and a powerful friend, 75-year-old Lord Chief Justice John Popham, organized friends and relatives in southwestern England and in London to ask King James to give them Virginia for colonies.

He did. One charter created two companies, the North Virginia of Plymouth and the South Virginia of London. It divided the land from Maine to the Cape Fear River between them—northern Virginia for the fish and furs group, southern Virginia for the commerce-agriculture group. Merchants of London, Plymouth, and Bristol accepted invitations to join the companies, share the royal grant, and pour in money, ships, office facilities, and organizing skill.

Five months after James's great seal was stamped on the charter in April 1606, the Plymouth group sent one of Waymouth's Indians, Chief Nahanada, back to Maine's coast to help Capts. Martin Pring and Thomas Hanham select a colony site. In London, the brother company took no time for such caution. Three ships left in December for the James River with 100 men, including John Smith, and four boys.

In early summer of 1607, settlers left Plymouth for the site chosen in Maine. "One company member said a hundred of those settlers were 'pressed to that enterprise,'" Sylvia Sherman told me. "Many historians interpret that to mean that Justice Popham sentenced men to America instead of to jail. Twenty gentlemen came too, and Skidwarres, another of Waymouth's Indians."

In mid-August they arrived at narrow, craggy Monhegan Island. They found the 12-mile strip of water between it and the Maine coast thick with an amazing number of fish—a discovery that would shortly make Monhegan the biggest center of English fishing next to Newfoundland.

Skidwarres led a boat party headed by Raleigh Gilbert, nephew of Sir Walter, across the 12 miles to Chief Nahanada's village on Pemaquid peninsula. Nahanada directed them to the site he, Pring, and Hanham had selected near the mouth of the Kennebec a few miles south.

At Popham Point, Sylvia and I waded in knee-deep snow to a flat, low ledge beside the Kennebec, the "official likely spot for the fort," Sylvia said.

"This has been a mild winter," she added. "But the settlers had the bad luck to run into one of our hard ones." It was hard everywhere in 1607. In London, the Thames froze so solid that an ice carnival was set up on the river. In mid-December at Sagadahoc, more than half the men quit, leaving in the last ship returning to England. The remaining 45 completed the fort, set up 12 cannons, finished perhaps 24 houses, a church, a storehouse, and "a pretty Pynnace . . . called the Virginia."

By February, colony leader George Popham, nephew of the Lord Chief Justice, old, ailing, and "of unwieldy body," had died. Troubles with the unruly settlers and easily disgruntled Indians apparently multiplied under 25-year-old Raleigh Gilbert, usually described as headstrong and poor in judgment. Although none of the settlers' accounts mentions quarreling and disobedience, Indians and French later told how the Abnakis once rushed through unguarded gates, killed several men, and drove the others out of the fort for a short time. One of several accounts adds that the Indians strewed gunpowder about, not knowing what else to do with it, and when it accidentally caught fire, some buildings were burned. In the dire cold, the men were "wondrously distressed." A food shortage "caused fear of mutiny."

In May 1608, a supply ship arrived with news of the death of Justice Popham, their chief financial support. In September, another supply ship brought news that Gilbert's brother had died and the young man was inheriting "a faire portion of land." He decided to go home. With no leader, no mines found, and the fear that every Maine winter would "freeze the heart," all the men clamored to leave too.

"Wherefore they all ymbarqued," some of them on the tiny Virginia. One account indicates they took a parting cannon shot at watching Indians, and this was the end of that "northerne colony upon the river Sagadahoc." At home, investors indignant at their unexpected return gave the company no more money for settlements.

But the Maine coast was not abandoned. Every season, fishing vessels by the score hovered around Monhegan Island. Crews dried their catches there and on Pemaquid's shores, and eventually built shacks to live in through the winters. A fur trade began. Monhegan-Pemaquid became as well known to southwestern England as Jamestown did to London.

John Smith, who had long since left Jamestown, summered on Monhegan in 1614, and while his garden grew he mapped the coast down to Cape Cod, naming the area "New England." His map included Patuxet, a harbor his patron Prince Charles insisted on calling Plymouth — English names in place of Indian names would make the land seem less strange to prospective settlers, he reasoned.

Smith's map, the death of thousands of New England's Indians from smallpox, measles, and pneumonia brought by explorers and fishermen, and the presence of the Maine fishermen's well-stocked ships only 150 miles from Plymouth made possible the survival of a group of Pilgrims there in 1620.

"But that's 13 years after Jamestown," I said to Sylvia at Augusta's airport. I would fly south to the James River to find out how Sagadahoc's brother settlers had managed to plant an English village permanently in the New World wilderness.

Holding on
In Virginia and Canada
1607 ★ 1620

Pistol pointed toward the circle of warriors, young Capt. John Smith held his Indian guide as a shield. He stepped slowly backward through sodden, icy grass. Arrows flew around him; one struck him in the thigh.

In this oozy woods near the source of the Chickahominy River of Virginia, 200 Pamunkey Indians slipped from tree to tree as the stocky, red-bearded man backed away. His hostage called out: "He is a *werowance* — a chief! He wants only to depart in peace!" Voices shouted back: The white chief would not die if he threw away the weapon that had already killed two of them.

John Smith did not trust their mercy. Promises might change in an instant to violence should they gain the advantage. "They are inconstant in everie thing, but what feare constraineth them to keepe," the 27-year-old Smith knew. If he could reach his canoe on the Chickahominy — so close he had heard his two companions' death cries minutes before — he might have a chance to escape.

Suddenly he felt one foot, then the other, slip into watery mud. He sank to his waist in the freezing mire, still gripping his hostage and holding his pistol high. The

John Smith, soldier, adventurer, and Virginia pioneer, mapped the Chesapeake Bay area and New England. Almost single-handedly he kept alive the Jamestown colony of 1607, England's first permanent New World foothold. His zeal and courage overcame wilderness dangers, hostile Indians — and quarrelsome settlers.

Indians darted closer, and waited. Half fainting from the cold, Smith at last threw away his weapon and surrendered.

Taken before Chief Opechancanough of the Pamunkey tribe, Smith quickly turned magician, playing for his life. From his pocket he took an ivory compass with a glass face. Amazement lit the chief's features as he handled it and listened to Smith's broken Algonquian describing the sun and stars, the earth, and its varied people. But after an hour, impatient warriors dragged Smith to a tree and tied him there. They nocked their arrows, looking to the chief for a signal. He held up the compass. John Smith would live.

Led from one Indian village to another during two bitter-cold weeks, Smith arrived in late December 1607 at Werowocomo on the lower York River, 12 miles north of Jamestown. In a longhouse there, Powhatan, emperor of a confederation of 8,000 Indians between the James and the Potomac rivers, waited for the captive.

As Smith entered, he heard a sudden shout—a salute to him, a chief—from the rows of men and women "with their heads and shoulders painted red." Tall Powhatan, about 60, draped in a great robe of raccoon skins, all the tails dangling, sat with two of his wives "upon a seat like a bedstead."

Food was brought to Smith. Powhatan studied him and talked with his advisers. What should they do with this white chief? Why had he and his people come here? What signs had the medicine men seen?

The parley ended. Some decision had been made.

John Smith saw two great stones brought in and laid before Powhatan. Abruptly, warriors grabbed the captain, dragged him to the stones, and pushed his head upon them. "[B]eing ready with their clubs to beat out [my] brains, Pocahontas the King's dearest daughter," a 12-year-old whom the captive scarcely had noticed, begged for his release. Her words had no effect, and in an instant she ran to him. She "got [my] head in her arms, and laid her own upon [mine] to save [me] from death...." A few days later Smith was back in Jamestown.

At the reconstructed Jamestown fort a mile upriver from the original site, I came upon a scene similar to the one John Smith saw on his return. "We think our thatched wattle-and-daub huts look like those the settlers built during the autumn of 1607," my guide told me. Jacqueline Taylor, of the Jamestown Foundation, had walked with me through an open woods of lofty pines, past the replica of an Indian longhouse, and around to the front of the log-palisade fort.

"The settlers had lived in tents within the fort all summer," Jackie said. "Almost every day, someone died. By September, more than 60 were dead of the 104 brought by Capt. Christopher Newport on three ships." Across the open slope by the river-bank the brightly painted replicas of the *Susan Constant, Godspeed,* and the tiny pinnace *Discovery* rested in deep shoreline water. Anchorage against the shore was a main reason for choosing the site. "Probably the men died from drinking brackish

Overleaf: With his Indian guide as a shield, John Smith fights off attackers by Virginia's Chickahominy River in December 1607. Mired in icy mud, wounded in the thigh, and "neere dead with cold," 27-year-old Smith finally threw away his gun. His captors dragged him out and, weeks later, took him before Powhatan, ruler of a confederation of tribes along the lower Chesapeake Bay.

creek water," Jackie added, "and eating poorly—a cup or two of wheat or barley a day, all that was left after their four-month ocean trip."

Heedlessness and indolence they died from, too, John Smith indicates. Their leaders wrangled about who should work; whether the Council President was eating more than his share; whether to keep a 24-hour watch against the Indians.

At the end of the summer the council replaced President Edward Wingfield with ailing John Ratcliffe, who allowed Smith to begin solving practical problems. In three months Smith had pressed to completion a number of huts, a storehouse, a church. He had made five daring excursions among the Indians, insisting with a show of guns that they barter corn, peas, pumpkins, and persimmons for "copper, beads, and such like trash."

Twice he arrived home with food just in time to fire the fort's cannon at deserters. They included even Wingfield and Ratcliffe, trying to steal off in the pinnace for Newfoundland. Stay or sink, Smith shouted at them. They stayed.

In early January 1608, just after his return from captivity by Powhatan, Smith saw most of his work go up in flames. Nearly 100 new settlers had arrived with Captain Newport the same day Smith came back, and through carelessness someone set the village afire. For the rest of the winter, so harsh the two-mile-wide James froze over almost from bank to bank, the settlers agonized in the charred ruins.

Newport and his crew, living aboard ship, stayed more than three months, loading their vessel with sparkly iron pyrites—fool's gold. Supplies dwindled. "Ever[y] once in four or five days, Pocahontas with her attendants brought . . . provision, that saved many of their lives. . . ." Even so, "more than half of us died," Smith said.

In April a ship brought supplies and 50 men. Smith set workers at rebuilding houses and planting corn. Then he escaped the arguing, lazing, and conniving for a summer of exploring the Virginia shore and Chesapeake Bay. Although he found no waterway to the Asian Ocean, he made a map that would be of incalculable value to seamen and colonizers for more than a century.

From reconstructed Jamestown, I drove over the bridge to Jamestown Island and walked to the edge of the river where a bronze statue of John Smith looks from its pedestal toward the fort's original site, now underwater. Storm clouds reflected darkly in the James; a fine drizzle began, reminding me of settlers' complaints of dampness, mists, fogs. Behind Smith I saw, among great cedars and low elderberry bushes, a bronze Pocahontas, forever running toward him.

Close by the Indian princess, I sat enthralled as I read accounts by John Smith and his eight collaborators. Assessed by present-day scholars as more truthful than historians once thought, *The Generall Historie of Virginia* for me filled the woods with cries and orations of disquieted Indians, mouthings and complaints of self-centered, impractical Englishmen. Above all rose the passionate voice of a Lincolnshire farmer's son, determined to keep the colony alive.

Returning from his Chesapeake mapping in September, Smith found "silly President" Ratcliffe deposed, and within a week was himself elected leader. He changed the shape of the fort from triangular to five-sided, drilled marksmen, restored guard duty. Then one October day, Captain Newport arrived with 70 new settlers, including the first two women, Mrs. Thomas Forrest and her maid, Anne Burras. Hired German and Polish glassmakers and carpenters came too.

*Condemned by Powhatan, Smith escapes execution as the Indian emperor's
12-year-old daughter, Pocahontas, protects him with her body. Granted his
freedom, Smith walked back to Jamestown, 12 miles away, but later returned to
Powhatan's village on the York River to barter for grain to feed his colony.*

But no food! Instead, Smith was handed a list of company directives "to make us
miserable." In response to an order to send back either a lump of gold, news of a
South Sea passage, or one of Roanoke's lost colonists, he wrote a heated letter of
rebuke. Another order—to crown Powhatan emperor and give him a fancy bedstead—he helped carry out, knowing it would make the old chief more arrogant. A
third—to load the ship with pitch, tar, sawed boards, soap ashes, and glass worth
£2,000 to pay for the voyage—brought forth more words of abuse and a token car-
go, much of it produced by his own blistered hands.

Then he set about to squeeze food from the Indians. It took a threat of war and
near-clashes, for Powhatan, alarmed at the number of white men arriving regularly,
had determined to starve them out.

Soon Powhatan decided the German carpenters, who had turned their backs on
Jamestown to live among the Indians, had a better idea: Kill John Smith and the
colony would die. An ambush in Powhatan's house was planned. But Pocahontas,
at the risk of her life, warned Smith.

A few days later, Smith saved himself from a plot at the longhouse of Opechancanough, the Pamunkey chief, by snatching in rage his "long lock [of hair]... pistol ready bent against his breast. Thus [I] led the trembling King... amongst all his people...." Smith raged at the astonished warriors, causing them to "cast down their arms." He took home the corn he wanted, paying for it with copper and beads.

Having risked his life for food, Smith had no intention of seeing it frittered away. He called a meeting and laid down the law to those "poor gentlemen, tradesmen, serving men, libertines and such like, ten times more fit to spoil a commonwealth than... begin one." He declared "that he that will not work shall not eat...."

After his ultimatum many became industrious, "yet more by punishment performed their business," he added.

But behind his back, guns and powder were taken from Jamestown to Powhatan by friends of the German deserters. "Kill Smith," the Germans persisted, and taught warriors to shoot guns.

One December day as Smith walked alone through the woods from glass factory to fort, he saw a chieftain making ready to fire at him. He "prevented his shot by grappling with him." The chief dragged him into the river. "Long [we] struggled in the water, till [I] got such a hold on his throat, [I] had near strangled [him]." Smith drew his sword to cut off the chief's head, relented, and took him prisoner. He soon escaped — and Smith burned his village, killed and captured many people, took boats and fishing weirs. The Indians made peace and bothered Smith and Jamestown no more. Powhatan, too, intimidated, left the fierce, bushy-bearded man and his 200 settlers alone.

For three months — February, March, April 1609 — Jamestown thrived, humming with industry: 20 houses built; 40 more acres of land cleared and planted; 8 tons of tar, pitch, and soap ashes produced and barreled; a well dug inside the fort; nets and weirs made; glass blown; clapboard and wainscot sawed. Chickens increased to 500; pigs to 600 — so many they were boated to nearby Hog Island to root and breed.

Then, a new disaster! Late in April, the colonists discovered that rats, thousands of them, and dampness had destroyed most of the stored corn. "This did drive us all to our wits' end," said Smith. He acted at once, sending a large group downriver to live on oysters, others to net fish, and still others upriver for whatever they could find. Most came back empty-handed, ready to grumble about root-flour bread and sturgeon offered them. Smith's wrath struck them when they pressed him to trade guns and tools for fruit the Indians brought. "He that gathereth not every day as much as I do," he exploded, "the next day shall be set beyond the river, and be banished from the fort as a drone."

They cried at Smith to abandon Jamestown, but he would not. A few ran away to Indian villages, but Powhatan's people also applied Smith's law — he who works not eats not — "till they were near starved indeed" and came home.

The ten-week emergency ended when an unexpected ship captained by Samuel Argall, on his way to fish at Monhegan, stopped at Jamestown. Argall had "wine and much other good provision," which Smith bought on credit. Argall also had news. The South Virginia Company of London had been reorganized and was sending supplies, more settlers, and a titled governor, Lord De la Warr, who would have the single-handed power Smith had found so necessary.

In London, power in the company had been (Continued on page 91)

*Creatures of the strange New World appear in the watercolors of John White,
first English illustrator in America. In 1585 White sailed to Virginia—then
a vast wilderness stretching from Maine to Spanish Florida—and spent a year
at Roanoke Island, where England first attempted a colony. During that year,
White rendered more than 60 detailed watercolors. Shown here: a terrapin,
brown pelican, land crab, and tiger swallowtail butterfly. White also captured
ways of life among the Indians. Published in 1590 by engraver Theodore de Bry,
White's works gave Europeans a remarkably accurate portrayal of America.*

Alcatraſſa. *This fowle is of the greatnes of a Swanne, and of the same forme saving the heade, w[ch] is in length 16 ynches.*

Tanboril.

A lande Crab.

SWALLOW-TAIL BUTTERFLY (no. 108A, cf. pls. 76(a), 90(c), 117(b), 160(a))

"At a certain time of the year the savages hold a great and solemn feast at which all their neighbors from the adjoining towns assemble. They come dressed in very strange fashion, wearing marks on their backs signifying the places they come from. They meet on a broad open plain enclosed by tall posts carved into faces.... Standing in a certain order, they dance and sing, making the strangest movements they can think of.

"Three of the most beautiful virgins, their arms about each other, turn around and around in the center."

—Colonist Thomas Hariot, describing Virginia Indians depicted by John White.

Their rype corne.

Their greene corne.

Corne newly sprong.

Their sitting at meate.

The place of solemne prayer.

The house wherin the Tombe of their Herounds standeth.

SECOTON

A Ceremony in their prayers w
strange iestures and songes dansing
abowt posts carued on the topps
lyke mens faces.

similarly concentrated in one officer, treasurer Sir Thomas Smith, guided by a company council more practical-minded than the royal one.

I searched out the small street in London where 50-year-old Sir Thomas, England's leading businessman, lived and ran the Virginia Company. To his house on Philpot Lane, near the old London Bridge, thousands of prospective colonists went to be interviewed during the decade after 1609. Here, too, money to support English colonization was collected from lords, knights, gentlemen, worthy citizens, guilds, societies—all responding to appeals from circular letters, pulpits, broadsides, and country-wide lotteries approved by the king.

For the 1609 shipment to Virginia, Sir Thomas assembled 500 or so colonists, including women and children. In May a fleet of nine ships set sail. One sank in a storm soon after leaving the harbor; another ran aground in the Bermuda Islands.

"What a shock to John Smith to see seven ships arriving in August with nearly 300 greenhorn settlers!" Parke Rouse, director of the Jamestown Foundation, told me. He described Smith's next desperate six weeks, ending with his departure from Jamestown forever. "Think of trying to house and feed that many people and keep an orderly camp. And all the while fighting for your job and even your life against plotting enemies. Remember that Ratcliffe and others Smith had sent home in disgrace were now back, and the company's temporary governor, Sir Thomas Gates, appeared lost with the ship that was wrecked in the Bermudas. Who should govern until De la Warr arrived—Smith or the newcomers?"

Gunpowder, exploding accidentally in Smith's canoe, decided the question. Severely injured, he went home, ending two and a half years in America's wilderness.

"Here at Jamestown, the worst happened," Rouse said. "They ate up their food and let up their defenses. By spring, only 59 remained; the others, about 430, 'being either starved . . . or cut off by the savages,' as Council President George Percy said. Incredible things occurred—cannibalism, Ratcliffe's death by Indian torture."

Skin-and-bones survivors crept out of the fort to meet two pinnaces in May 1610. Sir Thomas Gates and 150 men were at last arriving. They had spent nearly a year in the Bermudas building the small boats from their shattered vessel.

Gates quickly saw that his scant supplies could not keep Jamestown alive. After two weeks of listening to the men "accusing or excusing one another," all embarked "with the best means they could"—four small boats.

"Abandoning James Towne [we] set saile for England," a settler wrote. "But yet God would not so haue it, for ere wee left the river; we met the Lord de-la-Ware."

He ordered them back to Jamestown. By such a miraculous meeting of pinnaces and ships at the ocean's edge, the colony went on living.

Though colonists continued to sicken and die from fever, chills, and dysentery—only 150 of the 500 survived that winter—the Virginia Company somehow found more settlers and money to keep replenishing Jamestown. Martial law under Governors Gates and Sir Thomas Dale kept rigid discipline for five years, while in

John White's portrait of Secoton—one of many tidewater villages like those of Powhatan—compresses the growing season and Indian activities into one stylized scene: houses and fields, the central eating area, ceremonial rings marked by fire and dance. In a shelter amid "rype corne," one Indian could guard the crop.

Their ships at anchor, Jamestown colonists clear the land and build triangular James Fort. Tents and lean-tos within the palisades soon gave way to thatched wattle-and-daub houses. Within two years, additional homes stood outside the stockade, near fields of corn and wheat. But the first settlers on the swampy island, chosen for its deep shoreline water, suffered cold, disease, and the enmity of Indians determined to starve them out. Of more than 480 settlers, only 59 lived through the winter of 1609. Starved and sick, the survivors almost abandoned the faltering colony, but it survived and eventually prospered as Virginia's first capital. Today's reconstruction of Jamestown (right) includes stocks like those used in punishing wrongdoers. The Ashmolean Museum of Oxford, England, preserves Powhatan's shell and deerskin robe (upper right).

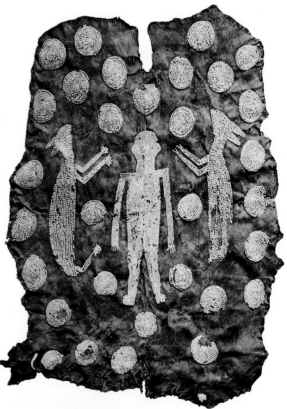

WALTER MEAYERS EDWARDS (BELOW); ASHMOLEAN MUSEUM, OXFORD

London Sir Thomas Smith tried to find skilled people of strong character to send to the primitive land.

In 1613, the incentive of a three-acre plot of land assigned by the Virginia Company for each colonist's private use coincided with John Rolfe's successful try at growing tobacco from seeds brought out of Trinidad and Venezuela. By 1616 the 324 settlers had tobacco fever. At Jamestown, the golden weed grew in the streets; in London it sold for six times the price of wheat.

During the same years, Powhatan lived in peace with the white men. Pocahontas, held hostage for a year by the settlers, loved the English, especially John Rolfe; her father consented to her marriage. In 1616, Mrs. Rolfe went to England with her husband and son. Smith, whom she had "always been told was dead," visited her, and her words to him strongly hinted that he had been her true love. A year later, as a ship started down the Thames to carry the ailing girl home to Virginia, she died and was buried at Gravesend near London.

Pocahontas's visit gave fresh sparkle to the name Virginia, long tarnished by grim stories or silence — many a friend or relative had gone there never to be heard from again. Before the excitement over Pocahontas wore off, the Virginia Company, now in competition for settlers with Bermuda, England's second permanent colony, offered free land. An emigrant paying his own way could have 50 acres, and for every head going with him, 50 more acres. Soon the offer went up to 100 acres, and groups could pool their land and send tenants to one big plantation.

Attractions increased as Sir Edwin Sandys, who gained control of the company in early 1619, publicized the decision to replace harsh Governor Dale with moderate Sir George Yeardley — and to allow Virginia its own Parliament. During the three years before 1620, growing numbers of settlers crossed the ocean to the James — and the land seemed to eat them. In mid-1619 when the first Legislative Assembly met in Jamestown's church, no more than a thousand survivors lived scattered along the river — the remnant of a total of six thousand who had come to settle.

In 1620, only the banks of the James meant England-in-America, and that year a thousand new settlers arrived. One group of a hundred Pilgrims planned to join them, but their storm-battered *Mayflower* landed instead in Massachusetts Bay. They would push English settlement half the distance from Jamestown to Quebec, where in 1608 Champlain had started the first permanent French settlement.

Champlain had spent a year in France after the pullout from Port Royal. About the time John Smith began his mapping of the Chesapeake, Champlain and a handful of settlers in two small ships began their Atlantic crossing. Sieur de Monts had a new fur monopoly for one year, and to assure himself of profits, he instructed his agent Champlain to settle where the fur trade was heaviest, on the St. Lawrence.

In early summer, Champlain was guiding his ship into Canada's sea-like waterway. Four hundred miles inside North America, he reached Tadoussac and beat off jealous countrymen, the Basques, who had for 60 years taken all the furs and whales there. About 150 miles farther, at Quebec — "where the river narrows" in Algonquian — he chose for a fur station the same wooded lower lip of the projecting rocky point where Cartier had found an Indian village 73 years before.

For the third time, Champlain supervised the building of a habitation for French settlers in America. At the base of the 165-foot sheer rock wall, and some 100 feet from the river's edge, sawyers cut beams and boards from new-felled trees. Carpenters hammered them into a large, closed circle of two-story row houses with balconies. A warehouse went up in the courtyard. Outside the enclosure, a forge was built, and land cleared for a large garden. That, except for a 1610 palisade, the slow addition of six private residences, a small convent, and some storage sheds, was Quebec for the next 35 years. Champlain, as much in love with America as John Smith had been, stayed on through endless changes of monopolists and company members. But hardly any settlers joined him.

"Fur merchants in Rouen, Dieppe, and other French ports didn't want settlers at Quebec," M. Roland-J. Auger, Quebec's genealogist, told me. "Settlers might start off as farmers and fishermen, but sooner or later they traded with the Indians on the side. That disturbed prices, took a cut out of the merchants' profits. So they sent only hired clerks, loyal to the company."

Roland walked with me to a small stone-paved square on the broad promontory where Quebec had begun. "On this square, Place Royale, Champlain's habitation stood," Roland said. "Now it's the center of a $30,000,000 restoration project—but to restore stone buildings built a century after Champlain."

"Actually, we have stronger links with the past than buildings," said Roland. "Many families, for example, are descended from Abraham Martin, a Scot who owned a farm called the Plains of Abraham. And every year in Quebec thousands of descendants of early settlers attend reunions—the Côtés, the Gagnons, the Héberts. I'm descended from Louis Hébert's daughter Guillemette. Champlain? He had no children. His wife, who brought him a large dowry, was 12 when they married in 1610. He was about 40. She stayed in France, and he spent most of his time in Quebec and on the sea, for he made a trip to France nearly every year for more than two decades."

In 1620 when Champlain brought his wife for a four-year stay, Quebec had grown from the 8 who survived the first winter to 46: six families, seven interpreters, eleven fur trader-clerks including Pont-Gravé, and a half-dozen missionaries.

From the first, Champlain's few settlers lived securely in the midst of thousands of nomadic Algonquian hunters and settled agricultural Hurons. As John Smith had tried vainly to persuade his council, the way to friendship with local Indians was to give them men with guns to help them fight tribal enemies. Champlain did, beginning shortly after his arrival.

With two settlers, he accompanied 60 Algonquians and Hurons south into the land of the Iroquois. They canoed and walked 200 miles along the St. Lawrence and Richelieu rivers until they reached a large lake, which Champlain named for himself. At its southern tip, the invaders found 200 fierce Iroquois ready for battle.

"The whole night was passed in dances and songs . . ." wrote Champlain. Shouted insults flew back and forth. At dawn the Iroquois attacked. Champlain, wearing metal armor, walked at the head of his war party to meet them. Only 30 steps from the Iroquois, he raised his arquebus, took aim, and fired. Two plumed chiefs fell dead. A third lay mortally wounded. Astonished at the deadly new weapon and its noise, the Iroquois "lost courage . . . and took to flight" as more shots boomed from the other two Frenchmen, who were concealed in the woods. It was a battle of momentous consequence. Overjoyed at this easy victory and others Champlain led them to, the Algonquians and Hurons pledged themselves to the French. For 150 years,

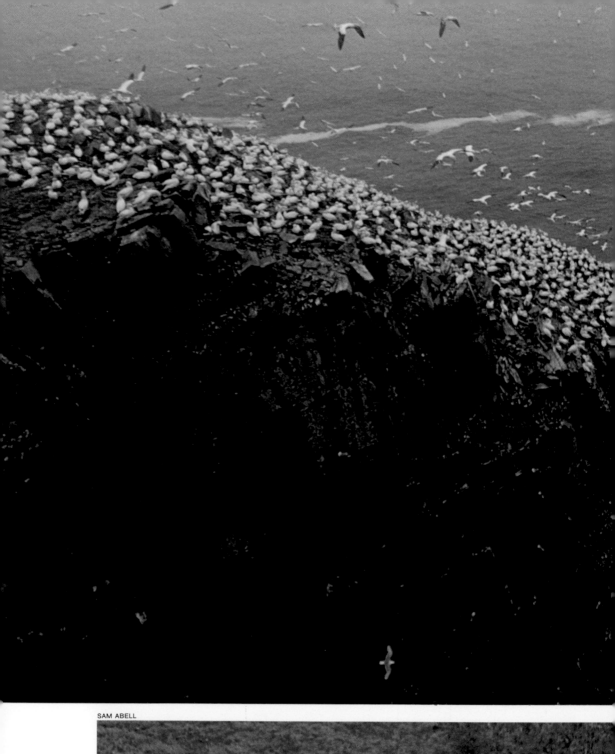

SAM ABELL

Blizzard of gannets whitens a crag on Newfoundland, where
caribou still follow ages-old migratory paths. America's vast
profusion of wildlife awed the early explorers. Today in
Newfoundland some animals, like the bear and the fox,
remain numerous. Others, the arctic hare, the marten, only
echo their former numbers. Some species, like the flightless
great auk that once blanketed the island's coasts, died out after
the arrival of Europeans bent on exploiting the wilderness.

Killing three Iroquois chiefs with one shot, Samuel de Champlain leads the attack in an intertribal battle beside the lake he named Champlain. This act, in 1609, firmly allied the "Father of New France" to the Iroquois' enemies — the Huron, Algonquian, and Montagnais who lived near his new village of Quebec. Artistic license permitted Champlain such inaccuracies as the palm trees.

until the last battles of the French and Indian War, a few French leading hundreds of warriors opposed English forces in the struggle over possession of Canada.

Quebec had a start and Champlain wanted to see it grow. Even against the deadly enemy scurvy, he had found a safeguard — eating fresh meat instead of dried, salted fish. After 1609 Quebec's settlers lived in tolerably good health through the winter, well-fed on corn and game bought from their Indian friends.

But Quebec did not grow for decades. Champlain begged for colonists from each new set of company merchants and each rich noble who bought the position of viceroy of Canada. But all refused to pay the transport and year's provisions for poor families, and no others would leave the comforts of France. Champlain felt lucky when he could persuade old friends like Louis Hébert, a Port Royal comrade, to bring his family and boost the colony by five people.

While the French held back, the English from king to company shareholders spread wondrous tales to lure thousands of families to America. Most settled at Jamestown — but a few hundred went to Newfoundland. Glorious promises blew into a colonizing bubble which produced puny, quick-shrinking settlements.

Left out of rival London's Jamestown venture, Bristol's merchants in 1610 were given Newfoundland by James I, responding to pleas of promoters like Sir Francis

Bacon. Quickly the new Bristol Company, led by fervent John Guy, advertised their new property as a land of lucrative profits. That same year Guy and 40 settlers landed at Cupid's Cove, about 50 miles north of St. John's.

They built ships, sold supplies to fishermen, and farmed, but profits didn't roll in. Shipbuilding in winter wore them out; fishermen ignored their attempts at rules and regulations, and began a century-long quarrel over sharing fish-drying beaches with houses and gardens. When I saw the rock-hard clay soil at the head of the mile-long narrow bay, I marveled that even a thin crop of oats was growing there.

"Bare subsistence," said historian Keith Matthews. "Not double wages or land grants—but no pay at all for 18 months. So, fed up, many settlers went home."

Their word-of-mouth complaints weighed little against the glowing letters of John Guy, and after him, Governor John Mason. They convinced another group of Bristol merchants to buy company land and round up hundreds of settlers for colonies north of Cupid's Cove at Harbour Grace and Bristol's Hope.

A rich, flamboyant Welshman, Sir William Vaughan, also bought land, sent two groups of settlers, then came himself. He and his colony manager, Capt. Richard Whitbourne, sent home praise so rapturous that King James ordered it read from every pulpit. Unsuspecting families signed to sail, and calculating rich men coveted a piece of Newfoundland. Vaughan sold quickly—before anyone learned he had gone broke and his settlements had shriveled.

One of Vaughan's customers was Sir George Calvert, later the first Lord Baltimore. Long cold months after he followed a group of men and women to Ferryland, a harbor a hundred miles south of St. John's, he was writing King James: "[I have] fowned by too deare bought experience which other men for their private interests always concealed from me . . . [that Newfoundland has] a sadd face of wynter." Lord Baltimore asked the king for land on Chesapeake Bay, a request that brought to the control of his heirs a huge grant that included present-day Maryland.

Like Lord Baltimore, John Mason took south his passion for colonizing America. He bought millions of New England acres, calling his 1622 tract Maine and his 1629 purchase New Hampshire.

By curious twists of events, Mason's settlement at Cupid's Cove played an important part in the success of another New England colony, Plymouth. In late 1614, a Patuxet Indian named Tisquantum, or Squanto, walked into the London office of John Slaney, manager of the Bristol Company. Slaney arranged passage for Squanto to Cupid's Cove on the spring supply ship.

No one knows for sure how Squanto came to Slaney's except that it was by way of Spain, where he somehow escaped after being sold into slavery by an English sea captain. Through Slaney, Squanto reached Newfoundland about 1617. From there in 1619 another captain, Thomas Dermer, took him to his old home at Patuxet—Plymouth. Squanto found no people: All his tribesmen had died of white man's diseases. But within months, the Pilgrims arrived and built houses on his old village site. Squanto, who had learned to speak English, joined them at Plymouth and for nearly two years stayed in the house of Governor William Bradford. Interpreter, guide, instructor to the Pilgrims in wilderness survival, and ambassador to Massasoit, chief of the Wampanoag Federation, he was, as Bradford called him, "a speciall instrument sent of God for their good beyond their expectations."

Pious Plymouth, Rowdy Manhattan
1620 ★ 1630

Alone in mid-ocean, the *Mayflower* dived into a swiftly rising wall of water. Black as the autumn sky and savage with gales and rain, the wave smashed across her deck. Wood cracked and splintered and a beam sagged like a half-snapped match, pulling deck boards with it. Water cascaded through to the lower deck, a new terror for the hundred crowded, bruised passengers. Clinging to bunks, ship's ribs, and each other, the Pilgrims prayed: "Yet, Lord, Thou canst save!" Twelve years earlier, their leaders had raised that same cry during a monstrous North Sea storm. Miraculously, their route from England to religious refuge in Holland had calmed. Another miracle now must save them on the way from Holland to the New World's distant shore.

Gray-haired Capt. Christopher Jones shouted orders. William Brewster and John Carver, with young William Bradford and Edward Winslow, hurried their eight Pilgrim families into the captain's cabin. With ship's cooper John Alden and army captain Miles Standish, they ran to help push boards against the fractured beam, trying futilely to press it up and together again.

"We brought a mighty screw to jack up heavy weights!" a voice called out, and a

New Amsterdam rowdy gallops full tilt in a game of "pulling the goose," reaching to yank free the prize by its greased head. Settled by Dutch in 1624, Manhattan Island soon harbored the drunken and profane of many nations, in sharp contrast to the piety of Plymouth, symbolized by the Bible above.

Cramped below deck on the Mayflower, *Pilgrims seeking religious freedom in Virginia endure a grim crossing of the North Atlantic in 1620. Contrary winds, storms, and continual leaks beset the ship. Its simply-attired passengers found it impractical to change clothes*

during the 66-day voyage; the cold sea provided their only wash water. Surviving on a diet of salted meat, hard biscuits, dried peas, and preserves, the Pilgrims dropped anchor in November off Cape Cod, far to the northeast of the Jamestown colony, their intended destination.

dozen men raced to find that iron muscle. Levering its heavy, spiraled rod, the men at last heard splinters crunch and mesh, saw beam and deck slowly rise into place. Later, the captain judged that the *Mayflower's* hull was safe and the journey would continue, despite entreaties by some members of his crew to turn back.

It had taken the 50 Separatist Pilgrims aboard the ship an agonizingly long time to reach this point in mid-ocean. For a decade after separating themselves from the Anglican church they despised, they had lived as exiles in Holland, along with about 250 other Separatists. There they spent three anxious years negotiating first with the Virginia Company, then with a sponsor offering land, ocean passage, supplies, and an agreement for them to pay later with products from America.

The sponsor, believing the band of Pilgrims too small for a colony, had recruited volunteers throughout England. Eventually, 102 passengers crowded aboard the 128-foot-long *Mayflower*. The recruits were "strangers" to the Pilgrims, faithful to the Church of England. They were not seeking religious freedom, as were the Separatist Pilgrims, but an opportunity to own land.

For days after the cracked beam was propped and the deck caulked, the *Mayflower* wallowed in the subsiding storm. Mistress Steven Hopkins gave birth to a boy, Oceanus. A youth nearly drowned when he slipped away from the below-deck stink of sanitary buckets, the cramped quarters, the oppressive tedium, and was thrown into the sea by the pitching ship. He grabbed a halyard as he fell, and was hauled back on board with a boathook.

Waves and wind gentle at last, sailors climbed rope ladders up the 45-foot mainmast and loosed the sails. Did Captain Jones know then that the *Mayflower* should turn south to reach Jamestown, its intended destination? For reasons never recorded, he held a westward course. At sunrise on November 9, the lookout at last sighted land—the clay highlands of Cape Cod, three weeks' sail northeast of Jamestown.

After the first hymns of joy, the settlers decided they should head south for the mouth of the Hudson River—just inside the boundary of the Virginia Company. Hollanders claimed that river too, but they were friends and had once asked the Separatists to go as New Netherland's first colonists.

Within a few hours, the *Mayflower* tangled with Nantucket's "deangerous shoulds and roring breakers." Wrote Bradford in his *History of Plimoth Plantation,* "Hapy [we were] to gett out of those dangers" when the ship turned back to Cape Cod.

On the way, "strangers amongst them" disturbed the leaders with "discontented and mutinous speeches." They declared that if they landed outside Virginia's boundaries, "none had power to command them [and] when they came a shore they would use thier owne libertie."

One stranger, Steven Hopkins, knew the dangers of such mutiny. Years before in the Bermudas, where Governor Gates and settlers bound for Jamestown had been shipwrecked, a similar rebellion nearly caused the death of all, himself among them. Pilgrims on cold Cape Cod could not risk such disorder.

Mayflower II, *replica of the Pilgrims' ship, rides at anchor at Plymouth, Massachusetts. In 1957 the English-built ship traced the voyage of the original* Mayflower *from Plymouth, England. The shallop alongside approximates the one used by settlers to explore Cape Cod before founding the Plymouth colony.*

In the few hours before the *Mayflower* landed, the Pilgrim leaders quickly wrote out a short statement of self-government that "might be...firme" and binding. Brewster, their reverend elder, Bradford, his young follower, Carver, their candidate for first governor, and Winslow all declared themselves combined "for our better ordering and preservation." Probably because of the persuasive skills of Brewster and Carver, 41 men, strangers as well as Pilgrims, signed the Mayflower Compact, pledging their families and servants to obey the colony's "just and equall lawes."

The last had hardly signed when the *Mayflower* anchored in the curve of Cape Cod's tip. Overjoyed, men and women and children "set their feete on the firme and stable earth" where Provincetown, Massachusetts, is today, and "fell upon their knees and blessed ye God of Heaven." But when they looked around, "What could they see but a hidious and desolate wilderness full of wild beasts and willd men," wrote Bradford. Behind them "a mighty ocean...to seperate them from all the civill parts of the world."

The area looked little better when Miles Standish led a wary party in battle armor to explore the sandy arm of land. To search out a site elsewhere they floated their storm-damaged shallop, after three weeks of repairing it in bone-chilling cold, and sailed along the shore. On the great bay they fought an icy storm which froze their clothes to them; nowhere could they find a harbor.

Suddenly a sailor's yell saved them from crashing into a reef. Wild waves and winds drove them past the rocks and into a broad, round harbor. They had arrived by chance in John Smith's Plimoth, Squanto's Patuxet, with its cleared fields and sparkling brook. Overnight and on the Lord's Day they rested on an island. "Ten of their principall men" and eight sailors stepped out of the shallop onto the mainland shore on December 21, 1620, a clear, sunny Monday. No written account mentions Plymouth Rock. That tradition started a hundred years later.

As the sun flickered through scudding clouds on a December day three and a half centuries later, I walked along the pier at the bottom of Leyden Street in Plymouth for a long look at the replica of the *Mayflower*. What other ship in American history evokes such wonder and affection? From April to Thanksgiving, schoolchildren clamber about her upper decks, squeeze through the cramped space below, and stare at wax-figure Pilgrims signing the Mayflower Compact.

From the *Mayflower,* I drove two miles to the reconstructed Pilgrim village. "We've made houses of hand-sawed boards," archeologist James Deetz said, "but the earliest might have been wattle and daub. In 1627 a Dutch visitor named Isaack de Rasieres said they were clapboard — 19 one-room houses and three public buildings. So far our digs have turned up no artifacts of the very early years.

"We do know that the first house was started on Christmas Day, which the Pilgrims didn't celebrate, finding no mention in the Bible of Christ's exact birthday."

During construction of the houses, the *Mayflower* lay at anchor a mile offshore, with most of its passengers ill with fever and tortured by scurvy. By mid-March, when enough houses had been built to allow the last settlers to leave the ship, 15 of 18 wives had died, as had 5 of 28 children.

Months with nothing to eat but salt meat, dried peas, and hard biscuits, and weeks of hard labor in pneumonia weather killed 19 of 29 hired men and servants, and half the 30 sailors. Only five Separatist family men lived — Carver, Bradford, Winslow,

Furnishings from New England's first colony survive in Plymouth. Flanked by a chair (left) that belonged to William Bradford and one used by Miles Standish, they include from left: Bradford's Bible, Standish's iron caldron, a cradle, and a mortar and pestle owned by ship's cooper John Alden. Today, Pilgrim Hall houses these artifacts, along with 17th-century wood-encased eyeglasses (below) and spectacles that came over on the Mayflower *with passenger Peter Browne.*

Brewster, Isaac Allerton—and eight strangers, Standish and Hopkins among them.

In the "depth of winter," only half a dozen stayed on their feet. Teenage Priscilla Mullins' entire family—mother, father, and brother—died. Brewster and Standish tended the sick, "fetched them woode . . . drest them meat . . . washed their lothsome cloaths without any grudging in the least, shewing herein their true love," wrote Bradford. Sailors who had sneered at the praying, talkative church folk, and strangers who had quarreled with them, now grew close in their suffering and personal grief.

The settlers' presence was known to the Indians, who had been watching furtively from the cover of the trees. On March 16, a tall, naked chief named Samoset strode up to their storehouse and greeted the astonished Pilgrims in broken English. Within a few days he brought Squanto who "could speake better English then him selfe," and Massasoit, the supreme chief of all the tribes from Narragansett Bay to Cape Cod. Impressed with the manners and goods of the Pilgrims, Massasoit signed a treaty which was to keep peace between the Indians and the white men for 54 years.

Squanto moved into Bradford's house. He showed the newcomers how to fish with weirs, how to plant fish as fertilizer with Indian corn kernels, how to snare deer.

The departure of the *Mayflower* in April 1621 left New England's first village of 50 colonists, half of them children, on its own. "We are well weaned from ye delicate milke of our mother countrie," declared Elder Brewster. Those who survived—widows and widowers—united. John Alden, without any recorded competition from Miles Standish, married Priscilla Mullins.

Summer work included a show of strength by Miles Standish and his soldiers to put the fear of guns into a few disgruntled Indians. And Winslow and Hopkins walked 40 miles to Massasoit's house in present-day Rhode Island for the chief's help in dispersing crowds of hungry Indians hanging around Plymouth.

In autumn, the settlers harvested good crops, killed scores of migrating geese and ducks, shot deer and wild turkeys, stored dried berries and plums, made wine from wild grapes. Bradford, governor since Carver's death in April, invited Massasoit to the Pilgrim's feast of thanksgiving. He came with 90 scantily clothed warriors, several husky inches taller than the white men, and for three October days all ate turkey and venison, pumpkin and corn, and played games of marksmanship. The Pilgrims competed with flintlocks, the Indians with bows and arrows.

It was a high point in the Pilgrims' American venture. Secure among Indian admirers, well-fed, provisioned for winter, comfortably housed, they had achieved their dream of living untroubled, saintly lives. The dream lasted about a month.

Beginning in November 1621 when 35 or so newcomers from England, mostly unruly "lusty yonge men," stepped ashore, bringing "not so much as a bisket-cake," a burden of people arrived every few months. Over the next two years they dragged the colony into periodic crises—quarrels, shortages of food and supplies, and crowded living space. With every page I turned of Bradford's account, I marveled as he did that the colony did not die or fall apart.

William Bradford, snared by an Indian deer trap on Cape Cod, suffered only surprise—and the laughter of fellow colonists. Lacking fresh water and a safe, deep harbor, the Pilgrims quit the Cape for Plymouth, where Bradford served as governor, holding firm to Pilgrim ideals that helped the colony endure.

In the spring of 1622, when famine "begane now to pinch them sore," a shallop brought seven more "rude fellows" by way of Maine's fishing camps. Winslow followed the shallop back and collected enough provisions from fishing ship captains to keep Plymouth alive. Yet some of the provisions and half the green ears of corn in fields worked by Plymouth women soon disappeared down the gullets of 60 summer-long drop-ins sent by Thomas Weston. His ruffians would not share their provisions "nor any thing els in recompence of any courtecie done them." Weston, the Pilgrims' major financier, had sent word to Bradford that he was "quit of" the colony because it made him no money. His intention now was to start a new settlement.

Leaving Plymouth even more exhausted and destitute, Weston's new colonists built cabins at Wessagusset, 25 miles up the coast at present-day Weymouth. Within weeks they'd eaten all their food. Winter's hunger drove them to the Indians for corn and meat, stealing, bartering, or even working at menial jobs. Riled Indians filched pots of cooking groundnuts or shellfish off their fires and contemptuously snatched blankets from sleeping settlers' backs.

Plymouth was saved when a trading ship happened by in the fall of 1622 and bought beaver skins for beads and knives which the Indians would take as pay for food. Hazarding a stormy sea, Bradford sailed to Cape Cod and brought home corn, beans, and venison. But he left his friend Squanto in his grave, a victim of fever.

Not long afterward, grateful for an English cure for his own grievous illness, Massasoit told Winslow that Weston's men would be "all knokt in the head shortly" and Plymouth attacked by warriors over whom Massasoit had no control. Miles Standish and his eight-man army promptly marched to the warriors' rendezvous, caught the leaders alone, and knifed three to death in a fight. As a warning to others, Pilgrim soldiers returned displaying a bloody Indian head atop a pike.

Weston's men cleared out of Wessagusset for Monhegan. Weston himself had just arrived. Soon he headed for Plymouth and was shipwrecked and "striped . . . out of all his cloaths to his shirte" by Indians. Although the Pilgrims, even in their own straitened circumstances, gave him 100 beaver skins to refit a ship, he went home mouthing malice to their new sponsors. "He could now set them all togeather by the ears," he said, for he felt they should have made him rich.

Actually, he left Plymouth's people working day and night just to find food while grain and vegetable crops grew. Bradford organized "6. or 7. to a gangg" to fish continuously, hunters to range the woods, women and children to dig shellfish. In midsummer, a seven-week drought parched the crops and distraught settlers stopped work for a day of prayers. A saving rain fell by suppertime.

The colony lived. But some of the 60 settlers arriving at the end of July in 1623 wept at the sight of the lean, ragged Pilgrims and "wished themselves in England againe." At least they brought provisions and, after that third harvest, Plymouth began to eat well and even had surplus food to trade.

From the third Pilgrim harvest to the next, however, three sets of problem people arriving from England dragged the village through a year of purgatory. Certain of the newcomers, "corrupte and noughty," were shipped home by Bradford's council, but only after splitting Plymouth into squabbling factions.

Adding to the turmoil, 50 men, women, and children crowded Plymouth for weeks while their leader, son of their sponsor Sir Ferdinando Gorges, searched the coast for a colony site. They vigorously disputed Plymouth's religion and rules and, after Bradford suspected them of setting a four-house fire, huffed off to Wessagusset's empty cabins. In early spring, most of Gorges' group quit the country.

Plymouth slowly grew and prospered. Winslow, Bradford, and Brewster led in building a trading house beyond Monhegan a hundred miles up the present-day Kennebec River in Maine. Corn and English goods bought Indian beaver skins for paying debts in England. Providence whispered no warning of yet another menace: Isaac Allerton, Brewster's son-in-law, was wasting their hard work and profits. Commissioned as an agent of the Pilgrims and sent to London, he received all their furs. But instead of selling the furs to pay off their debts, Allerton borrowed money on them himself to invest in trading and fishing ventures, "play[ing] his owne game." When the Pilgrims asked for an accounting, he confessed to "grosse miscarrages." The colonists dismissed him, but not before he left them with eight times their old debts at 30 to 50 percent interest. Years later, to finish paying them, Winslow and Thomas Prence sold their houses; and Bradford, Standish, and Alden sold land.

In 1627, on a day in autumn, Plymouth's families greeted a boatload of visiting neighbors from New Amsterdam, settled three years earlier on Manhattan Island, 200 miles west along the coast. "Accompanied with a noyse of trumpeters," William Bradford wrote, Isaack de Rasieres, commercial agent for the Dutch West India Company, stepped onto Plymouth's shore. In peacock-feathered hat, blousy knee breeches, waistcoat, and leather shoes with high heels, he looked his part as next in importance to the new settlement's governor, Peter Minuit. Behind de Rasieres walked Dutch and Belgian Walloon companions in wooden shoes, baggy pants, and plain coats. Separatists chattering in Dutch crowded around them.

De Rasieres in early 1627 had learned from the Indians exactly where to find Plymouth, and sent Indian runners with letters. Bradford answered that while Plymouth felt cordial toward their new neighbors, the English king wouldn't.

Eager to trade, de Rasieres ignored Bradford's warnings. In October, he arrived by ship in Buzzard's Bay at the Pilgrims' trading house at Manomet. An Indian ran 25 miles on to Plymouth with a note. "I fear my feet will fail me," de Rasieres wrote, and requested a boat ride to Plymouth on a creek across Cape Cod's neck.

After several days, Bradford accompanied de Rasieres back to Buzzard's Bay to see the goods he'd brought. Both wrote accounts of the occasion. Bradford dwelled on buying wampum, or seawan—a form of clamshell money for Indian trade. With a six-foot string worth a beaver skin, it became colony currency by 1630. But de Rasieres admired Plymouth's neat plank houses, the blockhouse with six cannons on the roof and meeting room below to which villagers marched like a column of soldiers. The community had not a single tavern or drunken Indian.

De Rasieres could only return to crumbly earthen Fort Amsterdam, a village of bark huts and a few row houses, underground rooms, a stone countinghouse, but no church for 300 people. "Rough and unrestrained" hired hands mostly, they worked at drinking and revelry, paying little attention to farming and building.

On open grassy acres cleared long before by Indians at the southwestern tip of narrow Manhattan Island's 12-mile length, the first hundred or so arrivals camped briefly in May 1624. Protestant Walloons speaking ancient French, they had signed up to live six years in the wild country.

Dutch toehold in America, the port of New Amsterdam had burgeoned with row houses and a rapidly expanding population as early as the 1650's (above). Some 30 years before, planner Kryn Fredericksz had envisioned the colony guarded by a huge fort (below). But his ideas never materialized, largely because the Dutch West India Company put profits ahead of expenditures for such defenses.

But the Dutch West India Company wanted fur-trading posts, and only a dozen settlers were left on Manhattan. A dozen others sailed north to the wilderness of the Fresh River, now the Connecticut; another dozen went to the South River, now the Delaware, to build trading shacks. All the rest, perhaps 75, sailed 145 miles north up the Mauritius River, today's Hudson, to build Fort Orange.

Breeding stock arriving in ships named *Sheep* and *Cow* and *Horse* specially out-fitted for their comfort prompted the next year's 150 arrivals to move from their first choice of Nut (Governor's) Island to Manhattan's better grass. Engineer Kryn Fredericksz and Director Willem Verhulst surveyed village streets to fit a plan sketched in Amsterdam. Without waiting for Verhulst to buy the land from Indians, as instructed, the 30 families quickly put up boxy pole-and-bark houses.

"When Peter Minuit arrived the next spring, he seems to have brought a barrel or two of trinkets," historian Maud Esther Dilliard said when I visited her on Long Island. Dissatisfied settlers sent Verhulst home, and newly chosen Minuit called to-gether the Indian chiefs one summer day in 1626. Before them he spread 60 guil-ders' worth of trade goods—probably hatchets, cloth, metal pots, and bright beads. The Indians made their "X" on the sales agreement for all Manhattan's 22,000 acres.

"In those days, 60 guilders equaled 2,400 English cents," Maud said. "Today, Man-hattan land sells at a rate of about $24 a square inch."

Minuit hurried up the digging for earthen ramparts at present-day Battery Park and sent for his wife. In early 1627, news from Fort Orange told of a few settlers who had joined Indian friends to battle another tribe and had been killed, roasted, and eaten. Fearful of a general Indian uprising, Minuit called to his fortified village all settlers on the Mauritius, Fresh, and South Rivers, except 16 soldiers to guard Fort Orange. Overcrowded New Amsterdam had nearly 300 people.

"The village stank of garbage, privies, and the litter of roaming livestock," Maud told me. "Rowdies and Indians noised around the taverns. Just outside the village, settlers tended grain, vegetables, and flowers on boweries, or farms."

In New Amsterdam's early years, only the company agents had the right to trade for furs with the Indians or with Plymouth, or for tobacco from Jamestown. Few Dutchmen jumped at offers of an arduous sea trip to America to work at low pay on company farms. The company welcomed new settlers of any nationality—by 1640 18 languages were spoken in the town. Mostly rural or seafaring men, they lived outrageously, "a rough lot who have to be kept at work by force," wrote de Rasieres.

In 1629 the company's directors, "Their High Mightinesses," offered a plan to attract investment money and more settlers. Company members would be allowed to buy from the Indians large tracts of land along the Hudson. If a patroon, or land-owner, could hire and keep 50 people on his farm, the company would give him a land grant. Several grabbed at the offer. Only Kiliaen van Rensselaer, aging diamond merchant who directed his plantation from Amsterdam, succeeded in holding his.

On both sides of the Hudson by present-day Albany, then Fort Orange, Rens-selaer's nephew-agents, Wouter van Twiller and Arent van Curler, bought him near-ly three-quarters of a million acres. How many barrels of beads, hatchets, and cloth they must have paid for a farm 30 times the size of Manhattan!

In Albany, I was reminded that Dutch fur traders built trading-post forts there on a now-vanished island in 1610 and 1618, years before the Walloons built Fort

Orange on the river's west shore. William Tyrell, director of the New York State Historic Trust, answered a question: Why hadn't the fierce Iroquois killed the isolated handful of traders, Walloons, and Rensselaer men?

"On the bluffs called Tawassgunshee just north of Albany," he said, "the Dutch traders in 1618 went to a great council of chiefs who headed the Five Nations — Iroquois tribes organized into a brotherhood by Hiawatha in the 1500's. They and their subject tribes along the Hudson would sell furs only to the Dutch, they promised, while the Dutch would trade them guns and teach them to shoot and to make bullets and gunpowder. At last they could take full revenge on Canada's Algonquians and French for the killing of Iroquois chiefs by Champlain. So, while the Iroquois shot French and Algonquians, torturing captives and burning them at the stake, they left the Dutch alone."

I read the journal of a Dutchman believed to be Harmen van den Bogaert, who one cold winter in the 1630's went out of Fort Orange west along the Mohawk River, scouting for fur business among the Iroquois. For six weeks he and two companions snowshoed through the woods and cleared fields, passing one Indian village or "castle" after another, eating and sleeping in longhouses. Finally they arrived at a palisaded Oneida Iroquois town on a high hill. Rows of noisy, curious people "let us pass through them by the gate...at the top were standing three big wooden images, carved like men, and...three scalps fluttering in the wind...."

A council member, annoyed that the Dutch brought no presents, declared that "we were scoundrels, and were not worth anything because we paid not enough for their beaver skins." Harmen, irritated, blurted out that the councilman "was a scoundrel himself." A tense moment, for "forty six persons [were] seated near us... they could easily have caught us...and killed us without much trouble...."

But nobody made a move. The council member began to laugh, and said, "You must not grow so furious, for we are very glad that you came here."

Two days later, the Oneidas set a price of four hands of seawan and four of cloth for a beaver skin, gave Harmen a fur coat, and "shouted as hard as they could: 'Netho, netho, netho!' which means 'This is very well.'"

The Iroquois had become very attached to the easier life European goods allowed them — and to brandy. In a few years, when they had killed all the beavers in their country, they wiped out the Hurons and raided French canoes transporting furs on Lake Ontario and the St. Lawrence. For 50 years of Beaver Wars the Iroquois harried the French. In return, French and Algonquians raided New England border settlements, burning, killing, and kidnaping for ransom.

But the day came when an imported French army smashed into the tribes of Hiawatha. Surviving Iroquois began to swing back and forth between French and English as each made bigger and bigger attacks in attempting to drive the other out of the continent. Dangerous, undependable, the Iroquois killed for the side paying the most, their love for the white intruders being no thicker than brandy.

Juncture of Canada's Saguenay River and the broad St. Lawrence seems untouched since Jacques Cartier saw it in 1535. Here, French fur hunters set up a trading post, Tadoussac, in 1603 and won over the Montagnais Indians. In later years English rivals swept through New France, taking over the land.

Lords Brethren and Lords Calvert
1625 ★ 1647

"Pemaquid, the next successful English settlement after Plymouth, is a lost story rather than a lost colony," archeologist Helen Camp told me as we stood at the empty site, a remote beach on a point of land in the bay-size mouth of Maine's Pemaquid River. "It lasted for more than 60 years but unfortunately had no William Bradford or John Smith to write the story of its early settlement."

Only wilderness loner Samuel Maverick, who had settled on Boston Harbor after a short stay at Wessagusset, recorded the colony's beginnings—with a single sentence. In his book, *A Briefe Discription of New England,* he wrote: "[In Pemaquid] Alderman Alworth of Bristole setled a Company of People in the yeare 1625, which Plantation hath continued and many Families are now settled there."

The settlers, numbering perhaps two hundred, started a village that prospered largely by providing homes and food and repairing equipment for the fishermen who sailed to the Pemaquid-Monhegan Island area every year. During its decades of existence, the colony survived an attack by the pirate Dixey Bull, and in the 1670's endured Indian raids in the war waged against the white intruders by King Philip,

Marauding Indian slays Mistress Anne Hutchinson, who helped establish Rhode Island settlements after the Massachusetts Bay Colony banished her for heresy. Puritans viewed her death in 1643 as "God's judgment." Such nonconformist colonists helped plant English settlements throughout New England.

son of Massasoit. But luck ran out for Pemaquid in 1689 when 500 French and Indian raiders burned its buildings and killed or captured its people.

On the coast halfway between Pemaquid and Plymouth lay another settlement begun a year after Pemaquid. I learned its story at the reconstructed Pioneer Village in Salem, Massachusetts. There, under giant seaside oaks and shaggy spruces, I saw plank cottages and dugouts and "English wigwams"—bent saplings sheathed with tree bark—all reminiscent of Naumkeag, as Salem was first called. Naumkeag was founded by Roger Conant, son of a Devon farmer, and about 25 companions as a result of the colonizing zeal of the Reverend John White and of merchants and clergy of Dorchester, England. They opened the way, through Salem, for the great Puritan migration.

In 1624 White and 118 Dorchester merchants and clergy pooled their money and sent fishermen—who they hoped might also do some farming—to rocky, stormy Cape Ann. After three years of big losses, the merchants called it quits. Their men at Cape Ann boarded ships for home. But one ship brought a letter from White asking Conant and a few men to hang on, so they moved south to warmer Naumkeag.

White rounded up new supporters in southwest England and secured a grant for a larger tract of land called Massachusetts. The Puritan Earl of Warwick, a London officer of the council that owned all New England by the King's charter, arranged it, probably without telling Sir Ferdinando Gorges, a powerful member of the council who lived in Plymouth, England. White now had a stronger argument for a Puritan refuge in America: King Charles I was punishing Puritans in Parliament for holding back on money for his royal pleasure.

Finally, in 1628, White's new company, now enlarged with men of wealth in London and the eastern counties, sent a ship carrying 50 workers and a new governor, army Capt. John Endecott, to Naumkeag, where Conant's group somehow had managed to hang on for two years. The next year 300 more workers arrived. They were to begin building "convenient howsing" for the Puritan migration.

But most of the workers fell sick. "Many dyed," Bradford wrote, "some of ye scurvie, other of an infectious feaovre.... Upon which occasion [Endecott] write hither for some help." From Plymouth, Bradford sent Samuel Fuller, self-taught doctor and ardent Separatist. Fuller must have worked without sleep, both to tend the sick and to talk religion with Endecott and Naumkeag's Puritan minister, for when he left he had radically changed their views.

Endecott wrote to Bradford: "I am by [Fuller] satisfied touching your judgment of ye outward forme of Gods worshipe." Moderate Puritan White doubtless was appalled when he learned that Endecott had set up a church like that of the radical Separatists. Its congregation, not England's bishops, would decide its rules.

Like Plymouth's Separatists, Endecott insisted that all Naumkeag obey the rules or get out. Soon, Roger Conant and his small group of Anglicans reacted to the demand for absolute conformity as many another would in the next decades. They moved. Two miles away at Beverly, across Naumkeag Bay, Conant's colony put up a wigwam village in the wilderness to house their own opinions.

In England, White's company had grown in influence. It had nearly 90 members, including dozens of aristocrats, landowners, and men of the professions. By the beginning of 1629 they had discovered a dismaying fact: part of Massachusetts

Quenching his thirst at a spring, so tradition says, John Winthrop makes a decision: He and his followers will build here. Ten years later, in 1640, their Puritan settlement, Boston, had grown to a town of 1,200; about 20 villages ringed the spiritual and commercial hub of the Massachusetts Bay Colony.

already belonged to others, among them Ferdinando Gorges' deceased son Robert.

The Puritans feared that one day Gorges would find out they were on land he could lay claim to and insist on taking control and collecting rents. They had to act quickly and secretly. They needed a royal charter that overrode that of Gorges. Puritans with connections at court called on the king's ministers.

The money they must have paid those ministers! I thought as I read an account quoting Matthew Cradock, a company leader. Cradock himself put it more decorously: "With great cost, favor of personages of note, and much labor," the Puritans obtained the king's great seal on their company charter. Massachusetts was theirs for a trading venture—not a word about religion.

The charter, dated March 4, 1629, created the Massachusetts Bay Company. Written by the Puritans, it gave company officers the right to rule the colony. The king didn't notice, and no one pointed out, that the rules failed to include the usual provision that the charter remain in London, where the king could revoke it simply by retrieving it and tearing it up, as he had that of the Virginia Company.

Within weeks, Charles I had dissolved the Puritan-dominated Parliament, and the company leaders had decided to speed up a secret migration of Puritans to America. They would send charter and officers 3,000 miles out of the king's reach. John Winthrop, 42-year-old London lawyer and a squire of Groton, Suffolk, agreed to go to Massachusetts as governor and to take the charter in his baggage.

Winthrop, intensely religious, capable, and persuasive, would have in America the public career denied him at home. In the New World, Winthrop could also rebuild his dwindling fortune with free land, and escape England's severe depression, hunger riots, and uncontrolled crime.

I read a copy of circulars sent privately to hundreds of Puritan groups in England, listing "provisions needfull for such as intend to plant themselves in New England, for one whole yeare—Victuells, Apparells, Tooles, Building materials, Armes." With the circulars went a compelling leaflet entitled "Reasons for Migration." By early 1630 many landed gentry, a few of them titled (Continued on page 124)

Snow-clad spruces cluster on Pemaquid Point in Maine, rendezvous of fishermen since the ear

600's. On its shore, they dried cod and mackerel—a source of supply for the English colonies.

SAM ABELL

Bleak but bountiful in fish, Newfoundland sustains coastal populations today
as it did centuries ago when fishing fleets sailed here to harvest cod, salmon, and
herring. Gradually, seasonal settlements built by fishermen became permanent
settlements. Today, profits from seals, hunted for their skins and for oil, still
supplement the earnings of local fishermen. Berries coated with ice evoke Lord
George Calvert's plea to Charles I in 1629 "to shift to some other warmer climate
of this new world, where the wynters be shorter and lesse vigorous." The English
king heeded his request, granting the House of Calvert ten million acres that
"shall be called Mariland in memory and honor of the Queene," Henrietta Maria.

In an idealized version of the founding of Maryland, Indians greet Leonard Calvert and his 200 settlers at the mouth of the Potomac River in 1634. A Jesuit priest celebrates the first Mass in the colony, conceived as a haven for English and Irish Catholics. Later, the Toleration Act guaranteed established policy: No Christian should "be any ways troubled" for "his or her religion."

aristocrats, had quietly paid their passage. Others had signed for free passage. Cautiously, they gathered at the ports of Southampton, Bristol, and Plymouth. To avoid attracting attention, they left at intervals for Naumkeag—a total at summer's end of nearly 1,000 on 16 ships.

Winthrop arrived at Naumkeag in June and took over from Endecott. He found only a few wigwams and dugouts, and in them men who were sick and weak. Nearby lay 80 graves.

After five days of exhausting discussion, mostly about the church—which had refused him communion because he wasn't a member of the congregation—Winthrop and other leaders decided Naumkeag "pleased us not." By boat, they went looking for a site that did.

Rounding Marblehead peninsula, Winthrop and his men followed the coast south and west for 15 miles, until they entered Boston Harbor. There they found two rivers, the Charles and the Mystic, and a hilly peninsula called Shawmut. Winthrop chose a site on the Mystic amid fields cleared by Indians long since gone.

But Winthrop's deputy governor, Thomas Dudley, insisted on having a look for himself. He promptly disapproved Winthrop's choice, and picked a site on the

Charles River that he liked better. After days of arguing, the two reached a compromise. They would settle on neither river, but at a place in between where Salem workers had built a few wigwams and a house near the thatched dwelling of blacksmith Thomas Walford and his family. Like Maverick, Walford had moved into the wilderness after leaving Wessagusset.

Soon ships and settlers moved from Salem to the compromise site, called Charles Town. Winthrop and the gentlemen occupied the house, and a tent city went up nearby. In the intense summer heat, garbage rotted, and water came only in cupfuls from a small spring. Dysentery and scurvy began killing dozens of men, women, and children. Hunger and anxiety grew as food supplies dwindled.

Suddenly a new threat arose. A sea captain thought he had seen French ships nearby. Demoralized, too weak to defend themselves, the Puritans divided into five groups—one to remain at Charles Town, four to hide inland in wigwam villages. Already a group had settled across the bay at Dorchester. At winter's end, all would reassemble to build a fortified town.

But the Puritans never built the town. They liked their new villages—Watertown up the Charles, Roxbury on Boston Harbor, Medford up the Mystic, and Saugus, halfway back to Salem. When spring came, they put up plank houses and churches where they were.

Winthrop had not considered bare Shawmut peninsula with its three high hills as a fit place for a settlement. Too small for farms, lacking trees for firewood, it jutted into the harbor in easy sight of any enemy ship. But in early autumn Winthrop left Charles Town to accept the invitation of the Reverend William Blaxton, another wilderness loner who had quit Wessagusset, to stay in his book-filled house on the west slope of Shawmut's highest hill. Winthrop's friends put up bark houses and tents near springs.

They named their camp Boston, for England's great Puritan city. Soon they moved their church, then the cannons, from Charles Town. Snows and meager fires gave Boston folk chilblains, but they wrote home that the camp had no "Woolves, Rattlesnakes, and Musketos." Scurvy abated when a ship arrived with casks of lemon juice.

In the other Puritan villages, the people had "all thinges to doe, as in the beginninge of the world," John Winthrop's son later wrote. Even men who had never set hand to labor before fell "to tearing up the Roots, and Bushes with their Howes."

Separated from England's bishops by an ocean, and from each other by miles of wilderness, each village organized its independent church. Congregations running their own affairs evolved from "New World necessity [and] the available models at Plymouth and Salem," historian Darrett B. Rutman says in *Winthrop's Boston*. Congregation business meetings had time added for town business meetings, and church leaders also serving as town leaders enforced the rules of both. In Boston, an annual assembly of a hundred or so freemen—church members of tested character selected by the leaders—elected the governor and his Court of Assistants.

Everyone, church member or not, was expected, and later required, to attend sermons and obey church-village rules.

Conant, Walford, and Blaxton refused to conform. Walford was expelled, Conant kept to his Anglican village, and Blaxton rode west into the wilderness on his white bull. "I came from England because I did not like the Lord Bishops," he

Victim of Boston's Puritan orthodoxy, Roger Williams winters with Narragansett Bay Indians in 1636. In the spring he established the Providence colony, based on religious freedom and the separation of church and state.

growled, "but I cannot join you because I would not be under the Lord Brethren."

I read the oath of office taken by the first assembly of villagers in the spring of 1631. They swore loyalty not to the king but to "the officers of Massachusetts," an action that amounted to a declaration of independence.

In England, tensions also heightened. The new head of the Anglican church, Archbishop of Canterbury William Laud, meted out new punishments there—dismissing and lashing ministers, cutting off ears, slashing nostrils, imposing jail sentences—to try to force the Puritans into submitting to rigid church control.

The Puritans balked. Prison and mutilation became more frequent punishments. Thousands of threatened people, including notables like John Cotton and his wealthy parishioners, in Boston, England, slipped away to ships anchored off lonely coasts, sails set for Massachusetts. About 200 shiploads made the trip over ten years. Estimates of the number of people range from 14,000 to 20,000.

Newcomers who were not servants expected land. Each year, the areas available for settlement were more distant from Boston. Although the rules decreed that settlers must build their houses in a village and walk to work on their farms, distance and wilderness forced separateness. Law enforcement became harder.

Winthrop and his Court of Assistants tried stronger laws. In Market Place they erected stocks, a whipping post, a cage for Sabbath breakers, and a gallows. In 1635 they required that new arrivals pass a test for Puritan orthodoxy, Boston brand, or return to England. Screening began the year the king revoked the company charter and authorized Ferdinando Gorges to go to Massachusetts as royal governor.

At last 70-year-old Gorges had revenge in sight. He had worked at it three years, ever since learning that the Puritans had been granted Massachusetts by royal charter. Gorges brought witnesses to the court of Charles I to prove that the Massachusetts Puritans were defying the king by making and enforcing their own laws. Charles was not impressed—until Gorges told him how the Puritans had slipped off with the royal charter and now swore loyalty only to their Massachusetts leaders. Furious, Charles declared the charter void. Gorges could go to Massachusetts, at his own expense, and restore the king's order.

If Gorges had reached Boston that year, 1635, Massachusetts might have fought our first battle for independence. Already forts with cannons and well-drilled militia guarded the town. Now the colonists had learned of Gorges' plans. On Shawmut's highest hill, thereafter called Beacon Hill, they placed a pole topped with a pot of tar ready for lighting an alarm if his ship appeared. I read Samuel Maverick's account of one jittery Sunday when the colonists thought Gorges had arrived. At the report that unidentified ships were approaching, "there was an alarme," wrote 28-year-old Maverick. "All the Trained Bands in Boston and Towns adjacent were in Armes in the streets...."

The ships came only from Plymouth, Massachusetts. Gorges' vessel, lavishly outfitted for a royal governor, lay useless in the harbor at Plymouth, England. It had toppled over while being launched. Gorges had no money to build another, and the king had none to spare. Rebellions at home took all his funds and time.

In America, Puritanism continued its headstrong way.

While Winthrop and his court tightened up their gates to keep Boston purely Puritan, astonishing news arrived from Jamestown. In the spring of 1634 two shiploads of settlers rumored to be Catholics had stopped at the James River on their way to settle on Chesapeake Bay, where Charles I had given "Mariland"—ten million acres of it—to a Catholic friend.

Had Boston's officials known that more than half the 200 settlers sent by Cecil Calvert, second Lord Baltimore, were poor Protestants and the others well-to-do Catholics, they might well have predicted failure for a colony tolerating such diverse views. Calvert had instructed the colony leader, his brother Leonard, to "treate the Protestants with as much mildness and favour as Justice will permitt."

On a flat point of land jutting into a small bay of the Potomac near that river's entry into the Chesapeake, I saw tiny St. Mary's City, capital of Maryland for its first 61 years, lazing under a warm September sun. Oyster boats were bringing in a rich harvest from the Chesapeake; tobacco barns on loamy farms were hanging full of drying tobacco.

However peacefully Calvert's Catholics and Protestants lived together, they carried on blood-stained fights on land and water with Virginia Anglicans on Kent Island far up the Chesapeake. Raids on the St. Mary's area followed take-overs of Kent during the years before Calvert gained and kept control of the island and the Indian trade on the bay.

While Calvert opened Maryland to all Christians, Massachusetts was exiling "heretics" — dissenters to its Puritanism. The Reverend Roger Williams, a young Welshman preaching in Salem, was the first minister to go.

To retrace his flight, I began driving one rainy September day south and west of Boston over a route that was once an Indian trail. With me was my son, James, a senior at the Massachusetts Institute of Technology in Cambridge. As we passed the red brick walls of Harvard University I noted that the college was started in 1636 to train preachers in approved Boston-Puritan thinking.

"That was the year Winthrop's court sent a man with a warrant to take Williams, who didn't preach approved thinking, and put him on a ship for England," I said. "But Williams was warned, and got away."

He trudged south through forests deep in January snow toward Sowam, the village of Indian chief Massasoit, an old friend from Plymouth days. Sowam probably stood where Warren, Rhode Island, is today, 50 miles southwest of Boston on the Palmer River near where it empties into Narragansett Bay. There Jamie and I stopped for an Indian supper of quahog clams and broiled young codfish, just as Williams might have had on his arrival, starving and half frozen. For three months he lived with the Indians in their "filthy smoke holes," as he described their houses. He learned their language, bought a piece of land ten miles or so north on the Seekonk arm of the Providence River, and canoed there in April. While he built shelters of saplings and boughs, a messenger took word of his whereabouts to his wife in Salem.

Among full-leafed maples, oaks, and willows, Mary Williams and her two children walked to Seekonk with three other families. Shortly Joshua Verin and William Arnold, ancestor of Benedict, followed.

"What awful thing did Williams say to get himself run off?" Jamie wanted to know. "He criticized Winthrop and his court," I replied, "and preached against a civil government run by church officials who used state power to impose their religious beliefs and rules of conduct on every citizen. Williams shocked them ('scared them,' Jamie inserted) with his picture of a commonwealth of Protestants, Catholics, Jews, Turks, praying or not praying, as conscience demanded."

In Providence some days later I stood on North Main Street, halfway up a high hill. Across a ravine gleamed the great marble dome of the state capitol. Bradford Swan, journalist and local historian, had brought me here after a visit to the site of Williams's clearing at Seekonk Cove, now in East Providence. "About the time their corn had come up there," Swan said, "Edward Winslow sent a letter to Williams from Plymouth, warning him to move to the other side of the river off Plymouth's land — or Boston would make big trouble for both of them. Williams canoed two miles down the Seekonk and found this slope beside Moshassuc River."

We walked uphill on the long narrow lot where Williams had lived a season in a

Into the lush Connecticut Valley, Puritan pastor Thomas Hooker leads his congregation to the site of Hartford in 1636. Two years earlier, his colonists petitioned the Massachusetts Court to quit the crowded Bay Colony. Lured by land, such emigrants thwarted Dutch expansion in the backcountry.

wigwam and tilled a small garden. "Williams was so poor that Winslow, on a visit that first summer, felt compelled to slip a piece of gold to Mrs. Williams," Swan said. "And Winthrop quietly sent them winter supplies, goats, and pigs."

Shortly after Williams and his followers settled Providence, a question of conscience upset the town meeting. Mrs. Joshua Verin's conscience bade her to go next door on weekdays to hear Williams preach. Joshua's conscience told him to make her stay at home and work. Whose conscience should the government support? The majority voted with Mrs. Verin, but Joshua's friend William Arnold jumped to his feet shouting that freedom of conscience should not extend to "the breach of any ordinance of God such as the subjugation of wives to their husbands!" Joshua packed up and marched his subdued wife into the wild.

But that incident was a mere spark compared with the fireworks four years later. Outcasts and refugees from Puritan towns arrived nearly every week in Providence. In 1638, just after Williams and his people had organized the first Baptist church in America, a trio of exiles came with a large following. Witty, egotistical Anne Hutchinson had for three years drawn bigger crowds in Boston than the famous theologian John Cotton. She interpreted *(Continued on page 134)*

NATIONAL GEOGRAPHIC PHOTOGRAPHER JAMES L. AMOS

Twisted fingers of Chesapeake Bay reach through forest and farmland on Maryland's Eastern Shore. Seventeenth-century settlers in the Middle Atlantic colony discovered a fertile land of gentle hills interlaced with inlets, bays, and rivers. Under the Lords Calvert, Maryland developed an economy built on tobacco; the Calverts themselves retained ownership of the land and collected small annual rents from the farmers. Today, shorebirds—among them skimmers (left) and egrets—still hunt the fishing grounds, among the richest in the world.

Cotton's intellectual sermons and spread widely her distorted Puritan theology. Banished after a long and noisy trial, she with her husband and her main supporters, former Boston councilman William Coddington and convicted heretic Samuel Gorton, sought a place of their own to settle. Roger Williams suggested a large island in Narragansett Bay, and helped them buy it from the Indians.

Mrs. Hutchinson, Coddington, and Gorton, in various combinations, revolted against each other periodically in their Rhode Island towns of Portsmouth and Newport. By the end of the second year, Gorton was revolting against everybody. Finally he was whipped and banished. He went to Providence.

That town barely survived his stay of 20 months. What should a tolerant community do with a turbulent character scoffing at laws, insulting officers, dividing the people into quarreling factions? They denied him the right to vote. He refused to go away. Disgusted citizens left instead, building a new village far down the bay at Pawtuxet. Those remaining in Providence took sides as incidents arose. Once even a gunfight broke out, and people lay dead in the street.

Gorton left, but to the dismay of the people who had moved to Pawtuxet, he and his admirers put up wigwams within quarreling distance. Pawtuxet appealed to Boston for help. Forty armed men marched from Boston to capture Gorton. A crowd of curious Indians followed the little army, watching the search for Gorton, the plunder of his village, and the fight to take him. In chains, Gorton and ten friends walked the 60 miles to Boston.

John Cotton gave them a long, admonishing sermon, and Gorton preached back, turning Cotton's Bible text into gibes. Public admiration saved Gorton and his men from hanging for heresy. Banished again, Gorton went to England to go over the Puritans' heads and get title to his land from the king.

Roger Williams, alarmed at Boston's long arm and aggressive hand, also went to England and appealed to the king. Both he and Gorton returned in triumph to their towns. In 1644, with a parliamentary safe-conduct pass, Williams retraced his walk from Boston through the wilderness, and at Seekonk Cove, Providence people in great processions of canoes joyfully accompanied him home.

Two years before Williams had fled from Boston in 1636, the rolling, forested hills in the Connecticut Valley some 60 miles northwest of Seekonk had reverberated with the sound of hammering and sawing, the lowing of plow oxen, the fall of ax blades on living wood. A cluster of three towns — Wethersfield, Hartford, and Windsor — soon housed a thousand people some 40 miles upstream from the sea. Thirty miles north of Hartford, a hundred more built Springfield.

"And don't leave out Fort Saybrook at the mouth of the Connecticut River," said Mrs. Marion Grant, a resident of the Borough of Fenwick in Old Saybrook, as we

Overleaf: First naval battle between colonists begins as Virginians and Marylanders clash on Chesapeake Bay in 1635. Virginia traders on the Cockatrice *raise arms and grappling irons while closing in on the* St. Margaret, *sent to protect Maryland waters for Governor Leonard Calvert. Three Virginians and one Marylander died in the beginning of a war over the bay and a lucrative trading base on Kent Island. For 12 years the colonists clashed, until Calvert established control of Indian trade on the bay.*

admired Long Island Sound from her front porch. "After all, Saybrook would have become Oliver Cromwell's home had he failed to win the Puritan civil war against Charles I. Now, 14 generations later, descendants of Lion Gardiner, the military engineer who helped build the fort, continue to live in a house on Gardiner's Island, off Saybrook. The island still has areas of virgin forest."

News of the grand and beautiful Connecticut Valley first spread through Massachusetts after Edward Winslow and a group of Plymouth men returned from a daring venture up the Dutch-claimed Fresh River in 1634. They had sailed boldly past the guns of Fort Good Hope, at present-day Hartford. "The Dutch threatened hard, yet they shoot not," Winslow reported. A few miles upriver they "clapped up" a ready-made house they had brought from Plymouth.

Soon they heard that the Fresh River Indians, the Quinnetukut, had died of smallpox caught from the Dutch. Word that the rich Indian land was now empty decided families in Dorchester, Watertown, Roxbury, and New Town (today's Cambridge) to sell their houses and lands to newly arrived Puritans and board ships for the Fresh River woods. From New Town, Thomas Hooker led a hundred people, most of New Town's population, on a two-week trek through wilderness to build Hartford.

In Connecticut, the newcomers laid out orderly villages next to the best land, and whacked a few Dutch soldiers on the head when they ordered that the plowing be stopped. "[You] Dutch have been here many years [and] done scarcely anything," one shouted at the soldiers. "[It's] a sin to let such rich land . . . lie uncultivated."

In 1636, Indian attacks made the settlers' problems with land titles and wolves seem small. Enraged Pequots, their canoes, wigwams, and crops destroyed by Boston men, besieged Fort Saybrook through spring and summer. In autumn, the Pequots asked the Narragansetts to join them in destroying all the white intruders in the valley.

When the news reached Winthrop, he turned for help to Roger Williams, who quickly responded and canoed alone in a storm to the Indian war council. Expecting every minute to have the Pequots' "bloody knives at my own throat," Williams spent three days persuading his Narragansett friends to shun the Pequots and join the English to do what Thomas Hooker called "this work of the Lord's revenge."

The alliance saved the Connecticut Valley towns, for in 1637 when the Pequots killed a dozen farmers, the towns formally declared war on the Indians. Connecticut and Massachusetts men, 90 strong, boated to the mouth of the Mystic River. Early one moonlit May morning, they stormed the village gates of the sleeping Pequots. Dazed Indians stumbled out of their huts, and the attackers ran them through with swords and rapiers. Capt. John Mason, commander of the attacking force, pitched a burning torch onto the mat roof of a wigwam.

"Standing close togeather, with ye wind, all was quickly on a flame," wrote eyewitness William Bradford. Captain Mason's men ran out the gates and killed Pequots trying to escape. Those who did slip past were clubbed by Narragansetts encircling the village. They "insult [ed] over their enimies in this their ruine and miserie," calling out, "O brave Pequents!" Bradford noted. Intense fire killed 700 trapped men, women, and children. "It was a fearfull sight to see them thus frying in ye fyer," Bradford recalled, ". . . but ye victory seemed a sweete sacrifice. . . ."

"Thus the Lord was pleased to smite our Enemies in the hinder parts," said Captain Mason, "and to give us their Land for an Inheritance."

Struggle Over Land, Rent and Rulers 1638 ★ 1699

"Big Belly," the Indians of New Sweden called him. In Wilmington, site of the Swedes' first town, I heard a Delaware jingle: *"Nobody before and nobody since has weighed as much as Johan Printz."* Four hundred pounds of governor! and all well larded with arrogance and ego.

Standing at the edge of a placid river on a ledge of rock near downtown Wilmington, I visualized a bulky Swedish ship approaching in 1643. It had sailed up the broad bay and into the Delaware River, then turned west into the Christina, where Fort Christina stood beside the natural stone wharf.

The ship anchors by the ledge. A few dozen Swedes and Finns on the wharf talk excitedly. Trumpets shrill, drums roll. Then everyone stares in amazement.

A giant seven feet tall, lumpy with fat and with floppy clothing, stands on the creaking gangplank. Then he leads into New Sweden his wife, son, and four daughters, his secretaries and artisans, and a hundred new settlers — slim, blond Swedes and chunky, dark-haired Finns.

Above Johan Printz's vast nose and chin, small icy blue eyes survey his capital: a

Tishcohan, Chief of the Delaware Indians, saw his people pushed from their ancestral homes as Quaker settlers, fleeing religious persecution in Europe, arrived in the river valley and pressed the Indians to sell their land. Tishcohan wears a squirrel-skin tobacco pouch in this portrait, painted from life in 1735.

few log cabins inside a log-and-earth wall. What a comedown for a colonel who once led cavalry charges for King Gustavus Adolphus!

Printz declined to live in the fort. He chose Tinicum Island, about 15 miles north on the Delaware, for his two-story log mansion, Printzhof. With glass windows, brick chimneys, paneled interior, and luxurious furnishings, it was the finest house between New Amsterdam a hundred miles northeast and Lord Calvert's village 175 miles southwest on the next bay, the Chesapeake.

I searched out Tinicum, empty and now attached to the mainland, about halfway between the Christina River and the Schuylkill, where Philadelphia later was built. As I traced out the house foundation in a lonely little park swarming with mosquitoes, I wondered how it happened that Scandinavians took this bay and river area already claimed by both Dutch and English, and in 1638 started building a colony. "The story began in Holland many years earlier with a Walloon named Willem Usselinx," curator Charles L. Seeburger explained to me at the American-Swedish Museum in Philadelphia. "Who these days has ever heard the name? Yet, his concepts and work started New Sweden."

Obsessed with the idea of colonizing in America, Usselinx gained the attention of the Swedish king. He convinced Gustavus Adolphus that a colony just south of Manhattan would produce furs, gold, and silver. Such riches would pay Sweden's army, fighting in the Thirty Years' War to free Protestant Germans from Catholic rule.

Prime Minister Axel Oxenstierna, Navy Minister Klas Fleming, nobles, clergy, businessmen, villagers, all joined Adolphus in pledging money to send settlers to America. But few paid—not even Adolphus—and no colony was organized. Years passed. The king died in battle and Usselinx died a worn-out dreamer.

"But his dream came to life again," Seeburger said. "Oxenstierna and Fleming in the 1630's formed a company with Dutch businessmen and hired Peter Minuit, dismissed years before as governor of New Amsterdam, to head the first expedition to America." The Swedes felt that New Amsterdam hadn't the strength of will or wealth to oppose a colony several days' walk or sail distant. They also knew that the English king, already on the brink of battle with Puritan armies, would do nothing to risk a foreign war.

In the spring of 1638, soldiers and artisans built their fort and named it for Sweden's new 11-year-old queen, Christina. Minuit bought the land from Indians. "Probably he paid even less for it than he paid for Manhattan," Seeburger said. Then Minuit took the artisans and sailed for Sweden to get more settlers. On the way, he died. In New Sweden's wilderness, two dozen Swedish and Dutch soldiers and a black slave waited two years before they saw another ship.

Their Indian neighbors liked them, for they paid lavishly in trade goods for furs—and security. Their Dutch neighbors, a few traders in a post by the Schuylkill, and a few soldiers at Fort Nassau across the Delaware, resented them. Furs now flowed to the newcomers, who seemed in control of the lower river and bay.

In Europe, Dutch partners in the venture, discouraged by Minuit's death and the lack of profit, sold out to the Swedes. Oxenstierna and Fleming grabbed Swedish army deserters, unfaithful husbands, poachers, and forest-dwelling Finns to ship to America. Despite five years of effort, they still had only a hundred unwilling settlers at Fort Christina when Big Belly arrived.

Disapproval clouds the face of Governor Johan Printz of New Sweden as he charges an English trader with bartering among Indians near Fort Christina in 1643. Though settled on land claimed by both Dutch and English, the Swedes held on to their colony from 1638 until 1655, when the Dutch ousted them.

"About half the settlers were Finns, sometimes called 'white Indians,'" Seeburger said. "In Finland and Sweden, they had lived in much the same style as the Indians in America." He showed me a museum mural with drawings of Finns living in huts of poles and tree bark, women pulling sledges, men in skin or fur clothing hunting deer with bows and arrows. "But when these nomadic Finns stayed in one place for a year or so, they built log cabins to live in and tiny log cabins for sauna bathing. So, when they came to the American wilderness, they built cabins in the woods—one-room with half-loft for sleeping and storage. Other settlers soon adopted the log cabin, which was sturdy, snug, and quickly built—better than wattle-and-daub."

Near Tinicum, at a mid-17th century log house built by a Finn named Morton, great grandfather of John Morton, a signer of the Declaration of Independence, keeper John J. Tisdale showed me how the logs were put together. "He axed four sides flat. Round logs didn't take as much work and time, but the mud chinking fell out faster. At the corners, notches dovetailed above and below for a tight hold." I asked about a cluster of nails driven into a log by the door. "To keep out witches," he explained. I had already read that nobody matched the Finns for numbers of witches, wizards, and sorcerers.

New Sweden lasted 17 years. During most of his decade there, Printz guarded an empire about 60 miles long on each side of the Delaware River, and laid claim to the bay. But with only a few soldiers in each of his six strongholds, he had to rely heavily on lying and bluffing to impress New Amsterdam Governor Peter Stuyvesant and Massachusetts Governor John Winthrop. While they, and the Virginians, sold Printz supplies, he drove off their infringing fur traders and bullied stray English settlers into paying him allegiance.

But after eight years his forces had dwindled to 80 soldiers. Five years had passed with no new people, no supplies. New Sweden's weakness eventually was found out and Printz's bluff called. In June 1651, Peter Stuyvesant sent 11 ships to the Delaware while he led 120 soldiers overland. Dutch vessels cannonaded up and down the river, moving Fort Nassau's guns to new Fort Casimir, just five miles south of Fort Christina. From Casimir the Dutch could shoot at any ship entering or leaving the river. Stuyvesant, enthusiastic about the site, called New Castle today, laid out the big village green himself.

Printz, no longer despot of the Delaware, drew in his scattered forces to Fort Christina, Printzhof, and the farms between. His empire had shrunk to 15 miles on one side of the river. When a group of his settlers handed him a petition demanding the right to trade at the Dutch store in Casimir, and accusing Printz of brutality, injustice, and greediness, he hanged the leader. Swedes and Finns ran away to Maryland and to the wilderness on the east side of the Delaware. In 1653, Big Belly packed up the riches he had collected, walked his family and servants through the woods to New Amsterdam, and took a ship for Sweden.

Probably while he was still at sea, 250 additional colonists arrived at Christina. Their impulsive new governor, Johan Rising, quickly struck at Dutch Fort Casimir and captured it without a shot. Incensed, Stuyvesant planned the end of New Sweden. In 1655, he led his soldiers and warships to Casimir and Christina. Again, no shot was fired while New Sweden became Dutch.

To their recaptured Delaware lands, the Dutch welcomed settlers of any kind. Within five years, a thousand Swedes, Dutch, and New Englanders had cleared hundreds of acres. They built houses, churches, courts. Wagon roads connected a number of wilderness villages. Lutherans, Calvinists, and Puritans lived to themselves, untroubled.

A decade passed. Then, England's restored monarch Charles II gave Dutch America to his brother the Duke of York and authorized a fleet to capture it. Warships filled with a thousand soldiers from England and New England trained their artillery on the town at the tip of Manhattan Island during the last week of August 1664.

Peter Stuyvesant stomped his wooden leg and raged. But trade-hungry merchants and officials in New Amsterdam, a restless mixture of 1,500 people speaking 18 different languages, begged for surrender. With few soldiers and no powder for the cannons, Stuyvesant gave up 33 settlements. Again, no shot was fired.

The new English governor, Col. Richard Nicolls, renamed the town New York. Down to the Delaware he sent ships to establish English rule over Dutch and Swedish villages. Now the English held all the east coast from Maine through Virginia and laid firm claim to the vacant land south to Spanish Florida. Just the year before, 1663, Charles had made a present of that huge tract — Carolina — to a group of friends, including Lord John Berkeley and Sir George Carteret.

In angry defiance, Governor Peter Stuyvesant of New Amsterdam shreds an English letter offering the Dutch lenient terms for the surrender of their lands on the Hudson River. But with few soldiers, and his own people against him, he yielded the colony in 1664 to the English, who promptly renamed it New York.

WILLIAM R. CURTSINGER

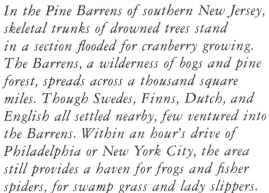

In the Pine Barrens of southern New Jersey, skeletal trunks of drowned trees stand in a section flooded for cranberry growing. The Barrens, a wilderness of bogs and pine forest, spreads across a thousand square miles. Though Swedes, Finns, Dutch, and English all settled nearby, few ventured into the Barrens. Within an hour's drive of Philadelphia or New York City, the area still provides a haven for frogs and fisher spiders, for swamp grass and lady slippers.

In Manhattan, Nicolls knew that the land west of the Hudson would put nothing in the Duke's purse until settlers turned forests into farms. Only a few score Dutch and Walloons lived in the Hudson River village of Bergen and on farms in the adjacent Weehawken and Hoboken areas. Nicolls sent enticing messages to New England towns, telling of rich bottomlands at no cost except a few goods and guns for the Indians, and almost full local freedom with no state taxes or religious restrictions.

Four Puritan families on Long Island responded quickly, and wintered in dugouts on the mainland across from Staten Island. In the spring of 1665, as they were nailing together plank houses, a shipload of strangers anchored at their landing.

Philip Carteret, in velvet, lace, and wig, led 30 relatives and servants ashore. He announced himself as governor of the whole area—five million acres—now to be called New Jersey. The Duke of York had made a gift of it to Carolina proprietors Lord John Berkeley and Philip's kinsman Sir George Carteret. They would make money not by gold mines or fur trade but by the flow of silver coin from the pockets of settlers. Land rents would begin in five years and continue "forever."

While Carteret's subjects pondered this dismaying news, the 26-year-old governor made a democratic gesture. He shouldered a hoe farmer-style and walked up the bank to his four-house capital, named Elizabeth Town for Sir George Carteret's wife. His retinue, from his home isle of Jersey, outnumbered the Puritan settlers.

"From Elizabeth Town, Carteret sent messengers to New England with copies of the proprietors' terms," I learned from John T. Cunningham, author of 14 books on New Jersey history. Religious tolerance and land deeded at no cost except for low annual rents had paid off for the Lords Calvert in Maryland, drawing 10,000 people there in 25 years. The lords in New Jersey would offer as good a deal or better.

During the next two years—1665 and 1666—five more New England groups moved to New Jersey. In the Elizabeth Town area, Puritans started Newark, Woodbridge, and Piscataway. In the Sandy Hook area to the southeast, Baptists built Middletown and Quakers began Shrewsbury.

"From the start, strong-minded, wilderness-hardened settlers, some within sight of Manhattan's windmills, gave New Jersey the makings of a contentious colony," Cunningham observed. I asked about the rebellion they staged.

"Which one?" he said with a laugh. "Well, they first rebelled just three years after the rent collections started, scaring Carteret back to England. Only Newark settlers had offered any payment, and Carteret refused that because it was grain, not silver. In May 1672 crowds assembled in Elizabeth Town. Talk rumbled about rents and the fact that Carteret had allowed his French-speaking servant—who was probably a Catholic as well—title to a house and lot. Puritans didn't tolerate tolerance, you know. In late afternoon, a dozen or so knocked down the servant's fence and trampled his garden. Carteret left town as crowds filled his front yard."

Angry Puritans, Quakers, Baptists, and Dutch found they could all agree about freeing themselves of absentee landowners, their governors, and rents. Organizing a government, colonists called a session of the Assembly, made laws, and elected "President of the Country" a chance visitor, young and easily flattered James Carteret, son of Sir George Carteret. James even wrote his father in support of the settlers' actions. Increasingly alarmed, Philip fled back to England.

A year later, the Dutch retook New York—without a shot—which ended New

Jersey rents and rebellions until the English took it back the following year, also without a shot. Philip Carteret returned to New Jersey willing to accept grain or any "country pay." The settlers brought nothing. Charles II threatened to seize their cows, wheat, and household goods, and most gave in. But rents and proprietors kept Jersey settlers balking for the next quarter of a century—until their sporadic, rowdy "Small Revolution" of 1700-1701 rid them of proprietors. "Good practice for the big one in '76," observed John Cunningham.

In 1674, in an effort to oust Carteret and to take back New Jersey for the Duke of York, New York's arrogant Governor Edmund Andros had Carteret dragged from bed and jailed, charging him with exercising unlawful jurisdiction. Carteret was acquitted, but Andros refused to let him return to Elizabeth Town until he agreed not to assume any authority there—a directive Carteret ignored. In the end, Andros's campaign of terror failed to regain for the duke any of the land he had grown to regret giving away.

George Fox, founder of the Society of Friends, probably sang the praises of Jersey land while visiting his aristocrat-convert, William Penn, in England, and urged him to invest in it when it came up for sale in 1673 and 1682. Fox had walked the length of New Jersey in early 1672 during a six-month preaching mission from Carolina to New York.

In all those regions his mellow voice and passionate words stirred a small revolution in religion. Fox declared that Christians needed no specially trained ministers, no special "priest houses, steeple houses." Christians should practice peace and brotherhood, never striking a blow, or swearing an oath, or engaging in lawsuits. He preached equality—of women to men, low class to high. He bade Friends not to remove their hats in respect to anyone, and to address lord and peasant alike familiarly as "thee" and "thou."

In England, infuriated officials confiscated the property of Quakers when they refused to tithe. They laughed at the simply dressed zealots quaking and moaning in public prayer. Then they beat, jailed, tortured, and occasionally hanged them. When 23-

Rush lamp flickers in the Old Dutch House museum in New Castle, Delaware. The wick— dried rushes soaked in grease— gives off a wavering light.

year-old William Penn became a Quaker, his father, an admiral and a friend of Charles II, beat him and barred him from the family's London mansion.

In 1656, the first Quaker missionaries to America, two women, arrived in Boston. "Heretics!" pronounced shocked Puritan ministers. "Witches," whispered the crowds in the street. The women were seized, stripped to the waist, lashed, and ordered to get out or be hanged.

They left, but more came—to Massachusetts, New Amsterdam, Maryland, Virginia. Often they were confined in stocks, branded in the hand with an "H" for

Coattails flapping, William Penn joins Delaware tribesmen in a dance at the Indian village Shackamaxon, now part of Philadelphia. The courtly appearance of the 38-year-old Quaker

elighted the Indians; his policy of paying for land kept them at peace. Before this visit in 1684,
enn wrote the Indians of his desire to "always live together as neighbors and friends."

147

heretic, shorn of their ears, starved in jails. Boston hanged two. Still, they would not stop preaching. "By 1660," says historian Rufus Jones, "southern Massachusetts was honeycombed with Quakerism."

And by 1665, they had Shrewsbury in East Jersey. After 1672, Fox's converts brought Quakerism into the politics of every English colony on the coast.

Just as William Penn was learning from Fox about New Jersey's richness and beauty he had a chance to own some of it. Quakers John Fenwick and Edward Byllinge had paid Lord Berkeley £1,000 for the lower half, which came to be known as West Jersey. The upper half became East Jersey. The buyers quarreled, and asked Penn to decide what each owned; the solution drew Penn in as a proprietor.

Retaining ownership of the land itself, the proprietors offered possession of farms in West Jersey to their Quaker brethren for a low cost and a small annual rent. Hundreds sailed yearly to the east bank of the Delaware. Swedes and Indians helped them become woodsmen. Shunning discord, 1,400 Quakers lived in 1681 on the 75 miles between present-day Trenton, and Salem in the south.

In Burlington, a village in between that was West Jersey's capital before 1700, I visited the area's oldest house, a one-room brick cottage with basement and loft, built in 1685. "To save it, I gave this lot to move it to," said Dr. Henry H. Bisbee. "I own one thirty-second of a proprietor's share, which entitles me to serve on the Board of Proprietors. The board was set up in 1688 to take over the details of distributing land—and it still functions."

Dr. Bisbee, a retired optometrist, told me that East Jersey also has a Board of Proprietors still in business. "It's in Perth Amboy, the old East Jersey capital. It lies by Staten Island, some 60 miles from here on a straight northeast line—along the New Jersey Turnpike.

"In the 17th century, that line would've skirted the upper edge of a million-acre sand and marshland area, mostly covered with pines rather than oak like the rest of Jersey. Settlers called it the Pine Barrens, and avoided it. A barrier between the upper and lower ends of the peninsula, the Barrens is still one of the biggest nearly vacant areas on the east coast."

Along the Delaware River where West Jersey's settlers farmed rich black soil, the Quaker towns in the 1670's adopted Penn's "Concessions and Agreements." A forerunner of the Constitution, it provided a democratic government, many guarantees of civil rights, and religious freedom.

In 1681, Charles II agreed to settle his debts to Penn's father by giving the son a 300-by-160-mile tract of wilderness across the Delaware from West Jersey. Penn wanted it named "Sylvania" but the king insisted on honoring Admiral Penn and made it "Pennsylvania," Penn's woodland.

About the same time, East Jersey was put up for sale at auction by Sir George Carteret's heirs. Of the 24 who bought it, half were Quakers, Penn among them. Although he could now collect rents from both Jerseys, his heart lay in Pennsylvania.

While Penn worked out a plan of government based on Quaker principles, wrote advertisements, and sold parcels of land, his agents in America searched the west bank of the wide Delaware for the best place to build a deepwater seaport. They chose a corner of land formed by the Schuylkill and the Delaware, about 100 miles from the Atlantic. Swedes already living there agreed to move.

"The Land floweth with Milk and Honey," wrote John Fenwick, who settled on Salem Creek in present-day New Jersey. But debts and quarrels over ownership of his holdings forced him in 1682 to turn the land over to William Penn.

By the time Penn himself came to America, in October 1682, his "City of Brotherly Love"—Philadelphia—had been laid out. In row houses along the riverfront lived a thousand English Quakers. When he left two years later, Penn could estimate the population at 4,000, including many German Rhinelanders, and the Swedes, Finns, Dutch, and New Englanders along the river. All paid him land rent.

Penn went home after seeing dozens of blocks of Philadelphia houses rising on farmlands cleared earlier by Indians and Swedes, after journeying on horseback to visit other governors and Quaker settlements, and after negotiating land purchases and peace with Indian chiefs. In England, he spent two worrisome decades wrestling like the other absentee proprietors with contentious colonists; in both Jerseys and in Pennsylvania they wanted complete control of their land and their government. Returning in 1699 for another two-year stay, Penn heard firsthand accounts of New Jersey's "Small Revolution" when time after time bands of settlers insulted, attacked, and jailed officials. Soon came Jersey's sale to the crown. But Penn would keep for his heirs Pennsylvania and the City of Brotherly Love, a prosperous port in 1700. In a few decades, largely through the efforts of the "peculiar Quakers," it would surpass Boston and New York to become America's social and political center.

Ardea cærulea

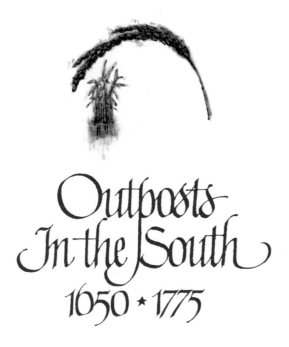

Outposts In the South 1650 · 1775

South to Carolina in search of converts journeyed Quaker George Fox. In October 1672, soon after arriving in Virginia from England, the powerfully built shoemaker-evangelist crossed the James River and paddled 15 miles down the Nansemond. He then jogged on horseback for two days along the "Virginia Road," a junglelike trail that skirted the western edge of the Great Dismal Swamp, 250,000 acres of thick murk, dark evergreens, and tangles of vines and briars. Notches chopped in tree trunks marked the way. "We were commonly wet to the Knees ... and lay abroad a-Nights in the Woods by a Fire," Fox recorded.

He was bound for the north shore of shallow Albemarle Sound, behind the Outer Banks, where five estuaries slice the land into a row of peninsulas. There 4,000 settlers, who had begun moving in during the 1650's, lived in log cabins widely scattered in deep forests of pine, oak, and cedar. Some had land grants from Virginia officials, but most had quietly disappeared from Virginia's tax rolls and slipped south to stake out a hundred acres or so of soft, black land in "Carolana," named for Charles I. Few of the settlers claimed any kind of religion; none had a church. They were good

Hand-colored etching of a little blue heron shows the lifelike detail of the work of Mark Catesby, whose portraits of American wildlife set a new style for realism in scientific illustration. Carolina rice growers welcomed the little blue herons because they ate burrowing crawfish that caused leaks in rice-field banks.

ENGRAVING BY MARK CATESBY, 1731, COLLECTION OF DR. AND MRS. GEORGE BENJAMIN GREEN; RIPENED GRAIN ARCHES ABOVE A CLUMP OF GROWING RICE (ABOVE)

On a Charles Town dock in Carolina, two wealthy traders watch the loading of a merchantma
with deerskins and barrels of pitch bound for England. Incoming vessels bring tools, woolens, and

...ther manufactured goods to the thriving colony. Under armed guard, manacled Stono Indian ...ptives await transport to a life of slavery on sugarcane plantations in the West Indies.

prospects for the Quakers' meet-at-home, every-man-a-preacher kind of worship.

Fox finally reached a lonely wharf inside the wide mouth of the Perquimans River, site of today's Hertford, North Carolina. For 18 days he spread the word of his new Society of Friends—and left so many converts that for 40 years Quakers and their sympathizers outnumbered all the region's other dissenters, as well as the Anglicans.

Quakers in the north part of Carolina, like those in West Jersey and Pennsylvania, dominated their government.

Carolina had been given in 1663 by Charles II to eight men for their loyalty to him during the decade that unfriendly Parliamentarians and Puritans kept him off the English throne. The land reached from south Virginia to the uncertain borders of Spanish Florida. By the time Fox arrived to convert the Albemarle settlers, their governor, Peter Carteret, had fled.

"Some of the country's cussedest folks lived in our backwoods," retired U. S. Coast Guard Capt. Nat Fulford told me after I had followed Fox's trail to Hertford. He drew a quick protest from Imogene Riddick, who, "like everybody else around here," is a descendant of early settlers.

"Well, their English and Virginia governors thought so," Captain Nat responded. "The settlers ran off four of the outsiders who were sent here to govern, two of them in armed rebellions. Mighty independent, those barefoot farmers. Like me. They had to be to survive. Used to doing what they pleased, nobody to bother them. When I said they were the cussedest, Imogene, I meant it as a compliment."

Between governors from London or Jamestown, local men led the settlers. An elected General Assembly and a General Court met regularly in family parlors until the first town, Bath, was built in 1705.

Most of Albemarle's early settlers were sons and daughters of parents born and reared in Virginia. Captain Nat and I discussed how a hard, isolated life had produced a new kind of frontiersman. Sun-browned, dressed in coonskin cap, leather moccasins, deerskin or homespun wool jacket and trousers, with flintlock in hand and corncob pipe in mouth, he looked and acted more like his Indian neighbor than his English grandfather. Alert eyes and steady hands, shrewd judgment and daring courage gave him status—not family name or education.

"Nobody got rich in Albemarle, and the life fell a lot short of elegant," Captain Nat concluded, "but the winter breezes in the pine needles are mostly warm. And living by the water—oh, it's grand. On my creek today, there came ducks and swans and geese, birds settling down by the thousands—prettiest sight I ever saw."

Of Carolina's eight owners, only three—Sir William Berkeley, Sir John Colleton, and Sir Anthony Ashley Cooper—took an active part in its settlement. Berkeley in Jamestown, as Governor of Virginia, organized the government and granted land titles in Albemarle. In 1665, a group of Colleton's friends in Barbados, an English island of sugarcane plantations in the southeastern Caribbean, came to live on the Cape Fear River in middle Carolina. Their colony lasted only two years. The settlers quarreled with the proprietors over land and taxes. Poor soil, late supply ships, and "vermin"—as the colonists called all tormentors, from Indians to mosquitoes—kept the people in poverty and misery. By October 1667, the settlers had abandoned the colony, walking through wildwoods and swamps 200 miles north to Albemarle, or crowding onto ships bound for Boston, Virginia, or Barbados.

Some months before the desertion of Cape Fear, a small exploring party sailed south to look for another site. Colonist Henry Woodward, 20, went along as ship's surgeon. On Port Royal, 250 miles below Cape Fear, they found a choice spot and friendly Indians. Woodward volunteered to remain with the Indians to study their island and their language, until his captain reported to Barbados and returned.

But not long after, Woodward was hauled aboard a Spanish ship as a prisoner and taken to St. Augustine. In 1668 he escaped with marauding pirates, who gave him passage to the Leeward Islands in the Caribbean. The next year he boarded a ship for London, only to be shipwrecked and washed ashore on the tiny island of Nevis, north of Barbados. Soon to that speck of land came two English ships and a sloop, putting in for water. Woodward, incredibly, found himself among old friends. The vessels carried settlers from England, Ireland, and Barbados, all bound for Port Royal.

In March 1670, after a three-year absence, Woodward again stepped ashore on Port Royal. He found his Indian friends gone, their village in ashes. Westo Indians living up the nearby Savannah River had taken the people as slaves, Woodward learned from a Kiawah chief. The chief persuaded the settlers to sail a day's journey north and live on his Kiawah River. He guided them to a bankside knoll 16 miles upstream from the river's mouth. There, in April of 1670, they built plank houses and a log palisade between the Indian village and a marshy creek. They first called their settlement Albemarle Point, but six months later they changed the name to Charles Town. The chief's river they renamed the Ashley, in honor of Sir Anthony Ashley Cooper, who had organized the expedition.

Almost immediately after completing the village, the 148 settlers were faced with the threat of a Spanish naval attack supported by Indian land forces slipping north from century-old Spanish coastal missions. A storm blew away the ships, and the Indians scattered. The expedition was the first of many attacks and harassments the settlers had to face alone during the next decades. For the town was hundreds of miles from other English colonies, a southern outpost lying, as one settler put it, "in the very chops of the Spaniards."

That first summer, friendly Kiawahs gave the newcomers venison, showed them oyster beds, and led them to the best hunting grounds for wild turkey. But enemies of the Kiawahs, among them the man-eating Westos, lurked in the woods; half the settlers stood guard while the others planted crops.

Before long, tempers began rising over land allotted according to a plan drawn by the proprietors in London. Some farms lay in watery stretches fit only for growing cattails. Absent proprietors and a few settlers flaunting purchased titles — "landgrave" and "cacique" — got the choice tracts. In August, the supply ship returning from Virginia brought orders from the proprietors. The colonists must load the ship with timber and anything else salable. The lords declared themselves "much out of purse" from financing the settlement and wanted immediate repayment "upon which . . . will depend the continuation of our supplies." Acting Governor Joseph West ignored the demands. In the next critical years, only the persistence of Lord Ashley in collecting and sending funds kept the colony in needed goods.

It was Henry Woodward with his knowledge of the Indians who found a rich source of income for the proprietors. In 1674 he began the first stage of opening up trade in the vast Indian territory to the west, arranging for the Westo Indians to furnish him with "deare skins, furrs and younge slaves." The proprietors offered Woodward a fifth of all they received and forbade Charles Town's merchants to trade in the western lands. For guns, liquor, and cloth, Woodward got huge stacks of deerskins. "There is such infinite Herds [of deer]," wrote one visitor, "that the whole Country seems but one continued Park." Secretly, the merchants' agents also dealt with the Westos, bartering mainly for their Spanish-Indian war captives—mostly women and children—to sell in slave markets of the West Indies and New England.

At the end of six years, the merchants had forced Woodward out and incited the Savannah Indians to exterminate the Westos. But Woodward returned from London in 1682 and opened up a new area of trade farther west and south, luring the Indians away from their Spanish allies. By that time the Charles Town colonists had moved their settlement ten miles downstream to an easily defended site with a better anchorage, where the Ashley and the Cooper rivers joined. On the docks of the new town Indian slaves by the hundred and deerskins by the thousand changed hands for sacks of shillings and were loaded aboard trading ships.

"But skins and slaves brought prosperity to only a few," historian Converse Clowse reminded me when I talked with him about Charles Town. "Most of the other settlers struggled along, raising livestock, tobacco, a little cotton, and silkworms. None of those turned into the high-yield export crop they were looking for."

Henry Woodward is often credited with introducing one about 1685—with a bag of Madagascar rice brought to him by a ship captain. "It grew well in open fields, and even better in swampy lowlands," Dr. Clowse said. By 1690 the planters had a surplus to sell, and the rice boom had begun.

So had the boom in African slaves, brought in to take over the drudgery of growing rice in a malaria-ridden country. The population of Charles Town and that of the river and coastal island villages and plantations doubled between 1690 and 1705, and most of the newcomers were blacks—4,000 of them. They and 1,400 Indians slaved for 4,000 whites.

Charles Town, rebuilt with brick after periodic fires and hurricanes, was thriving as the only English port in the far south. It outshone Virginia's new capital at Williamsburg and rivaled Boston, New York, and Philadelphia in trade, particularly with the nearby West Indies. But one day late in 1699 news reached the Charles Town merchants that the trading position of their 200 Indian agents in Alabama country was in peril. The French had built a fort on the Gulf of Mexico where the Biloxi Indians lived. Their leader was none other than Pierre le Moyne, Sieur d'Iberville, the Canadian terror of King William's War, a bitter struggle in the 1690's between the Canadians and the New Englanders that had ended in a draw.

Iberville, sent by Louis XIV to settle his lands, planned to throw the English traders out of the Gulf Coast area and attack the English colonies all along the Atlantic. Brilliant warship commander and battle strategist, Iberville and his 18-year-old brother Jean Baptiste, Sieur de Bienville, had set out with 200 settlers in February 1699 to scout the Gulf Coast in search of the mouth of the Mississippi. They knew that the entrance to America's mightiest river had eluded the great explorer La Salle 15 years before. He and his 200 settlers sailed past it and landed at present-day Matagorda Bay, Texas, where hostile Indians destroyed their colony.

Iberville and Bienville anchored their fleet at Ship Island and with 50 men took to birchbark canoes and longboats to find the river. During four days they threaded through rush and sedge, then tall cane. At last the land began to solidify and they paddled through swamps and bayous. Finally they reached the strong current of a wide river. Indians they met showed them a 13-year-old letter left for La Salle by his lieutenant, Tonti—proof that the river was indeed the Mississippi.

But the Frenchmen went a hundred miles upriver before they saw land high enough for a settlement. It lay in a great crescent-shaped bend. Bienville wanted to bring the settlers there, but Iberville doubted the place would survive high water. Young Bienville saw it as the site for a future city that would control all river traffic. Eighteen years later he would found a village there and call it Nouvelle Orléans.

Disappointed with the Mississippi, Iberville returned to Ship Island and began a slow, tedious sounding of the shallow water there. "Our provisions falling short," he wrote, "we thought it best to commence operations at the Bay of Biloxi. . . . merely on account of the roadstead." His Fort Maurepas, with Indian-style huts standing

"HARLEIAN MAP," KONINKLIJKE BIBLIOTHEEK, THE HAGUE

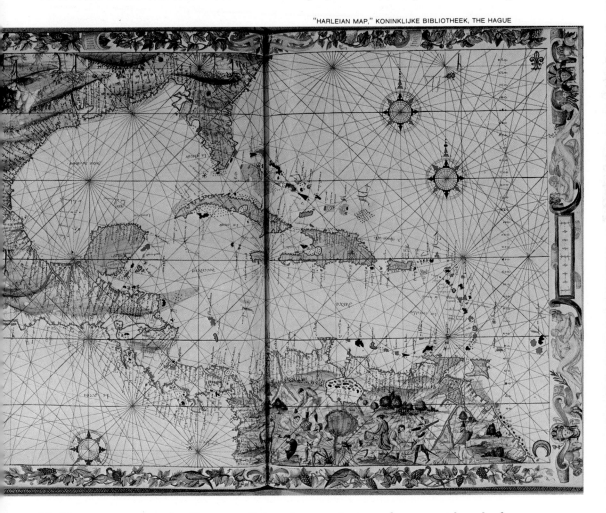

Half a century after the discovery of America, mariners and cartographers had blocked out, with reasonable accuracy, the main outlines of the Caribbean and the Gulf of Mexico. This ornate, unsigned map dates from the 1540's.

WALTER MEAYERS EDWARDS

Great Dismal Swamp lies equally divided between Virginia and North Carolina. Colonists quarreled for years about their boundary through it until Virginia's William Byrd II surveyed it in 1727. He described the swamp as a "dreadful place," its air so foul that "not even a turkey buzzard would fly over it." Bald cypresses (left and above) rear thick trunks and gnarled knees out of vegetation-stained waters.

Year-old Savannah, Georgia's first colony, shows meticulous planning in this 1734 engraving. Pleased to have fellow English settlers provide a buffer against Spanish Florida, Carolinians gave them horses, cattle, sheep, and money.

outside a log palisade, probably stood behind present-day Ocean Springs, Mississippi.

Iberville went to France for more settlers and supplies. Returning in 1700, he found many Biloxi colonists dead of fever. Survivors complained of an icy winter, hurricanes and hordes of mosquitoes in summer, wolves, bears, and no sign of gold. They grew no food, counting on supplies from home and eating Indian acorn bread when their own flour gave out. So many of the settlers from Canada had taken to the woods to hunt and trade with the Indians that Iberville wrote the king to send marriageable women "to anchor the roving *coureurs de bois* into sturdy colonists."

During that first year, young Bienville had scored boldly against the English. While exploring the Mississippi one day, he encountered a ship loaded with English settlers, convinced them they couldn't stay, and watched them depart from a bend in the river still called English Turn.

In 1702 Iberville, who had just brought a third load of settlers and supplies, again set sail for France, never to return. He left his brother in command of the new fort at Mobile Bay and in charge of a plan to lead the French, the Alabama country Indians, and the Spanish at St. Augustine in an attack on Charles Town. But Charles Town's men learned of the plan and struck first—at the Spanish. By the end of 1703, Carolinians had taken and occupied St. Augustine briefly and burned all the forts and mission villages of Georgia and western Florida, beheading and burning priests and soldiers, and enslaving the Indians. Mobile was to be next. Carolina traders in the area campaigned with low-cost goods to win away the Indian friends of the French. Bienville used French goods to buy them back. For a decade competing white agents led their Indian allies in the Alabama country to war against each other.

Mobile survived. Slowly the scattering of colonists in the area, including Canadian traders, grew to some 400. But discontented soldiers and ragged settlers, several dozen now married to young women sent from France, had cost Louis XIV a great deal of money and had sent him no gold or pearls. He turned all of Louisiana over to a businessman in 1713, expecting him to send gold miners. But four trouble-filled years later, the bankrupt businessman gave up. Few Frenchmen had consented to go.

"Lies, and one of history's most spectacular get-rich-quick land speculations — the Mississippi Bubble — turned the trick, bringing thousands of settlers to Louisiana," Joseph Tregle told me in New Orleans. Dr. Tregle, professor of history at the University of New Orleans, showed me a 1720 cartoon of John Law, the narrow-faced Scot gambler-playboy who started the Mississippi Bubble. Law happened to be in France when Louis XIV died in 1715, leaving the country near bankruptcy; to the nation's distraught ministers, Law sold his idea for restoring the economy. Create a state bank that would assume all the dead king's debts, he said; then pay the debts with paper money — a new idea — backed by the gold in Louisiana's undug mines! To dig the gold, send settlers. To pay their passage, sell stock.

When the stock went on the market in 1716, nobles sold estates, and peasants emptied their purses to buy, even after the stock soared to 60 times its original price. In 1720, after thousands of settlers had gone to Louisiana but no gold had come back, investors began redeeming paper for hard coin. There wasn't enough. Fortunes vanished in the panic. Law had to sneak out of Paris and run for his life.

"Well, at least those mad years brought settlers to Louisiana," Dr. Tregle said. "When few volunteers appeared, the stock company, desperate for 'miners,' took inmates out of prisons, orphanages, and asylums. That wasn't enough, so the company hired roving bandits, *bandoulliers de Mississippi,* to kidnap poor people, vagrants, prostitutes — anybody they happened to catch."

Even before that, the company flooded Europe with fanciful advertisements about rich, glorious Louisiana, a country "full of mines." Shiploads of Germans came, and Swiss, and Low Country people. Across the bay from Old Biloxi, where present-day Biloxi stands, John Law's agents had a big staging area. There newcomers made rafts to take them to their land. Ships left settlers with nothing but their valises, and many died of starvation and exposure.

Bienville now had settlers, such as they were, and in 1721 an engineer laid out his capital, Nouvelle Orléans. The town's immoral and generally worthless French harassed Bienville. But industrious Germans and practical Swiss settling near the capital went to work growing rice, indigo, and livestock. Villages appeared at Natchez and Baton Rouge on the Mississippi, and at Pineville far up the Red River.

Bienville's long struggle with the Carolina traders at his back door abated for a few years when in 1715 Charles Town was suddenly threatened with destruction. Ten thousand Yamassee and Creek Indian warriors, from tribes in the lands south of the colony, revolted. Before the Charles Town militia sent them fleeing to St. Augustine, 400 traders, planters, and villagers died.

But the three-nation battle for the southeastern corner of the continent soon resumed. Again, proxy armies of Indians did most of the fighting for Charles Town's 6,500 English, Florida's 1,000 Spaniards, and Louisiana's 6,000 French.

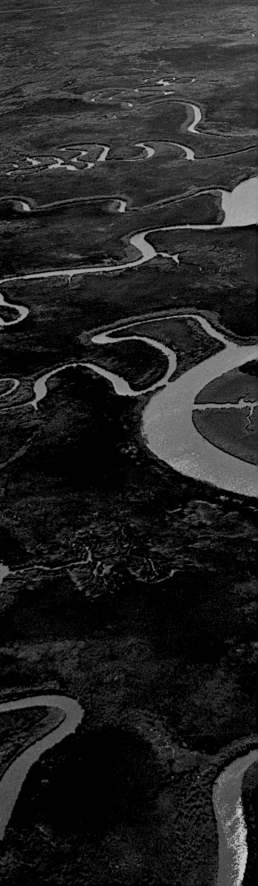

Fretwork of waterways in the
Mississippi River Delta flows toward
the Gulf of Mexico. French colonists
held this Louisiana coastland against
the Spanish and English, stamping
it with enduring Gallic culture.
Spanish moss beards trees along
duckweed-smothered bayous, and deer
splash through the wet wilderness.

DAN GURAVICH (RIGHT); THASE DANIEL

To the Mississippi area he governed on the Gulf Coast, Jean Baptiste, Sieur de Bienville, welcomes wives for his restless settlers—French peasant and orphan girls "reared in piety... who know how to work." This group, carrying their trousseaus in tiny chests, landed at Fort Mobile in the summer of 1704.

Near Charles Town, Spanish-allied Yamassees continually raided English farmers living on Georgia land that once was theirs. Apprehensive Charles Town men asked the proprietors for a new, well-armed colony to stand between the rich town and its Florida enemies. The proprietors refused. Charles Town evicted the governor with a show of cannon and in early 1720 declared itself under the rule of the king.

In the next decade, Charles Town got the Georgia colony it wanted. King George II, who had bought out the proprietors, sent Gen. James Oglethorpe with 114 settlers to the Savannah River. They arrived in early 1733.

The 35 families built a crane to lift their goods from the river's edge to the top of the steep embankment. In a letter sent to England at the end of January, Oglethorpe said: "I marked out the town and the common; half of the former is already cleared, and the first house was begun yesterday in the afternoon." From his damask-lined tent he directed the building of rough-hewn plank houses, all alike. His design called for two blocks of houses, then one block of open ground, repeated over and over. Twenty public parks with live oaks, magnolias, and flowering shrubs still give Savannah a downtown of unusual and pleasant distinction.

After traveling south from Charleston a hundred flat and marshy miles, I looked out over the wide, slow-moving Savannah River from a stone retaining wall 40 feet high which reinforces the face of the bluff where the town of Savannah was built. "From the key of the town you can see the [river's] whole course to the sea," 18 miles away, wrote Oglethorpe from that same spot.

"Savannah was to be a Utopia with communal living, no liquor, no slaves, and equal housing, farm acres, and opportunity," my guide, Catherine Webster, told me. "All the families — honest, upright, and poor — would make a living by growing silkworms, or cultivating grapes for wine."

Although the idea for a colony on the Savannah came from the Charles Town people, it took hold in England as an idealistic answer to a humanitarian problem that had arisen there. Curiously, Oglethorpe himself created the situation that caused the problem: After one of his friends died in debtor's prison, he agitated so much that his king, George II, let debtors go free; almost overnight, England had thousands of jobless people wandering about. What to do with them?

Led by Oglethorpe, a group of prominent men asked George II for land in Carolina where the debtors could go. Oglethorpe's plan caught fire in England, then on the continent after it was enlarged to include the persecuted. Charitable groups, clergy, merchants, nobles, and members of Parliament crusaded throughout England to collect money and equipment.

When a board of trustees began screening the thousands of applicants for the Savannah colony, it emphasized Charles Town's purpose — military. Construction engineers, masons, carpenters, and farmers chosen to go did weeks of gun drill with the guards of Buckingham Palace. Few freed debtors ever went to Georgia.

Oglethorpe, tall, austere, and 43 years old, left his soldier-settlers building their houses on the Savannah River bluff and went scouting the coastal islands. He picked sites for forts within 40 miles of St. Augustine. During the next few years he built them with money Parliament voted in the excitement of a visit he made to London in 1734 with a seven-foot-tall Indian friend, Chief Tomochichi.

Oglethorpe manned the forts with hardy fighters recruited in the Scottish Highlands, with stout English volunteers and, in a few years, with 600 British troops sent in a great, convoyed fleet. In 1739 three years of Spanish thrusts began, both by land and by sea. But they never quite succeeded in getting past the general's defenses.

In time, however, Utopia dissolved into Savannah grogshops, large land holdings supported by slave labor, quarreling settlers gathering furs instead of raising silkworms, and steady departures of Georgians for better prospects in other colonies. By 1743, when Oglethorpe left, the colony had dwindled from a peak of 5,000 to 500. King George, taking control from the Trustees in the 1750's, had to start over again and refound his colony.

The grand finale of the three-nation struggle for North America began in 1755 and was known to the American colonists as the French and Indian War. At its end, eight years later, the English flag flew in all the old French and Spanish lands east of the Mississippi, except for New Orleans.

George II left his son in possession of 13 colonies on the eastern coast. A million English settlers and 500,000 Negro slaves lived there. George III could rule and tax them as he pleased — or so he thought until 1776.

Across the continent meanwhile, in a nearly treeless coastal wilderness, Spanish settlers in heavy leather armor and in the long brown robes of priests hurriedly built stick-and-mud forts and missions. Until then, that remote land had been empty of European settlements. But ominous news from Russia abruptly set the Spanish running to stake out the coast before the Russians grabbed it first.

Missions and Fur Posts On the Pacific 1740 ★ 1841

Sea otter pelts, luxuriously thick, lay in high stacks on the crude boat floating into a small bay on the southeast coast of the Kamchatka Peninsula. Cossack Sgt. Emilian Basov and his 30 men shouted and waved to astonished fellow Siberian Russians ashore as they brought their treasure home to the village of Petropavlovsk.

In late summer of 1743 when Basov had set out, nobody expected to see him again. Only a madman would challenge the stormy North Pacific in a keelless, two-sail riverboat bound together with leather and caulked with moss and tree gum. But in a few weeks Basov was back, with enough furs to make him a millionaire.

He had found the island, 300 miles away in the Commander group, where explorer Vitus Bering had taken refuge from Arctic storms two winters before. Pelts brought out by Bering's men eloquently revealed that fortunes in sea otter filled the waters around numerous islands between Siberia and North America.

In Petropavlovsk, fortune seekers tied timbers into flatboats and followed Basov back to Bering's island. Across the Siberian steppes the cry of "Otter!" sounded to fur traders like the cry of "Gold!" to Spanish conquistadors. A fur rush began.

"I put a cross on the foreheads and breasts of six children," wrote Spain's Father Junípero Serra of Indian baptisms at San Luis Obispo in 1774. From 1769 to 1782 he saw the founding of nine missions on the San Diego-Monterey trail, carrying "the torch of civilization into the new land"—Alta California.

TLINGIT CEREMONIAL RATTLE (ABOVE)

Jagged rocks of the Monterey Peninsula jut into the Pacific. The adjoining bay served as the sit

for the Spanish capital of four presidio-missions — fortified settlements — guarding Alta California.

Brass plate, dated 1579, bears the name of Francis Drake. Almost 200 years before the Spanish occupied Alta California, Drake entered a harbor in or near San Francisco Bay. While there, he nailed a marker to a post, claiming the land for England. Some historians accept the plate above, found on San Francisco Bay in 1936, as authentic; others consider it a hoax.

Hunters killed all the otter around the Commanders, then worked the Aleutian chain leading 1,200 miles to the American mainland. They robbed and enslaved the Aleut Indians, taking the women and forcing the men to hunt sea mammals for their pelts. "God is high above and the Czar is far away," laughed the hunters.

On the Chinese border, the Russians traded otter pelts for Oriental tea, a necessity for every Russian samovar. Profits totaled millions of rubles a year.

In the mid-1760's Czarina Catherine the Great let slip to Spanish, English, and French diplomats in St. Petersburg the secret that Russians were in America. "She loved to startle the ambassadors and to boast of the exploits of her subjects," writes American historian Hector Chevigny. Catherine told of an expedition she was sending to America's western coast—failing to mention that it was only an exploring party. And she said nothing of the furs and the extravagant prices they were bringing from the Chinese, news that would have started a rush of rival fortune seekers.

But word of Catherine's "expedition" was enough to convince Charles III in Madrid that this time the Russians, long a rumored threat to his Alta California, were actually sending colonists to occupy the land.

"Spain for 200 years had claimed the west coast," historian Ray Brandes told me in San Diego, California. "But she did nothing with it, except let the Jesuits start more than a dozen poverty-ridden missions in the desertlands of Baja California.

"The name 'California?' No, it's not Indian," he said. "It's invented. When Cortés's men found Indians diving for pearls off Baja, they named it for a pearl-rich mythical island, California, widely known from a popular novel of the time."

More exploring proved Baja wasn't an island, as the Spanish first thought, and that Alta California lay walled off from Mexico by deserts and mountains — and by strong opposing winds and currents when approached by sea. Since Francisco Coronado's luckless search for gold, Alta California had seemed part of a vast worthless land. Even the beginning of a rich spice and silk trade between Mexico and the Philippines, with galleons returning on ocean currents that swept near Alta California's coast, shook no money out of the crown for a land base desperately needed for fresh food and water.

But Russian ships bringing settlers to start a base on that same coast was another matter. Hastily, Charles III wrote Mexico's Viceroy Marqués de Croix. The viceroy's swiftest horseman took the news to Visitor-General José de Gálvez, who was traveling in western Mexico. "I thought that [a Russian] invasion would be made by way of the famous port of Monterey," the viceroy wrote. He instructed Gálvez "to make an expedition by sea toward the threatened port."

Square-faced Gálvez, arrogant and ambitious, stretched his orders and determined to send men and goods by both land and sea.

In hot, dusty Loreto, presidio-mission capital of Baja, Gálvez labored a year, pulling together the essentials for the journeys and settlements. Luckily he found in Loreto two exceptional men to lead the expedition. Capt. Gaspar de Portolá, 46, governor of Baja, became convinced he hadn't a minute to lose to fortify Alta California against "the atrocities of the Russians, who were about to invade us." Franciscan Father Junípero Serra, 55, the new leader of Baja's missions, rejoiced at going to spread Christ's story among untouched tribes of aboriginals.

Ships and mule caravans, carrying about 300 men in all, left early in 1769 for San Diego, first bay above the long Baja peninsula. Portolá and Father Serra, with "leather-jacket" soldiers and Christian Indian workers, left last. Portolá observed the slight, fragile priest, wheezing with asthma and limping on infected foot and ulcerated leg, and wondered if he would live through the arduous journey. But fierce missionary zeal and astonishing physical endurance would carry the Majorcan-born padre far beyond Portolá in deeds, years, and fame in California.

Along Baja's east coast desert, they stripped the missions of the last shovel, Bible, cow, and mule for the new settlements. Beyond the northernmost mission, they suffered through arid mountains, desert rocks and dunes, and broiling days and freezing nights. Soon their water, food, and Christian Indians were gone. "We went on, lamenting," wrote Portolá, "now to the mountains to kill geese and rabbits, now to the beach for clams and small fish, and then in search of water."

Gunfire echoing in the hills on July 1 announced the approach of Portolá and Serra to those who had already arrived at San Diego Bay. "Great rejoicing!" Dr. Brandes exclaimed. We had driven from the Spanish-style arches and blue-tile dome of the University of San Diego to a hill overlooking the bay a mile distant. Near the top of the slope, old foundations newly uncovered by archeologists showed us where the Spaniards put up brush shelters and later built barracks of adobe. Pines and eucalyptus trees shaded the site. "Portolá saw few trees; nearly all California's coastal trees have been introduced here," Dr. Brandes observed.

Men in the shelters lay groaning with scurvy from their 110-day sea journey, and others lay faint with the exhaustion of a three-month's walk. Death and Indian runaways had cut the number of settlers in half. A herd of 400 cattle, laboriously herded a thousand miles, ran wild over the dry plain.

From the high slope, Portolá had a sweeping view of San Diego's wide oval bay. No Russian intruder could escape detection. "Father Serra and three other priests, including Father Juan Crespí, whose travel diaries made him famous, piled up brush into a temporary chapel and said Mass," Dr. Brandes said. Portolá's men, worn and thin but in better health than the rest, built a house and a chapel of vertical sticks plastered with mud and thatched with tule reeds.

Feeling the urgency to begin his search for Monterey, Portolá allowed only two weeks for building San Diego. Then with 62 men and a string of pack mules, he began the journey north near the coast. Monterey had been described in 1602 by Spanish explorer Sebastián Vizcaíno as a landlocked harbor "sheltered from all winds," and Portolá had this description firmly in mind.

Father Crespí's diary described the five-month trip. Villages of Indians "naked as Adam" welcomed them and their strange animal transports. Wide valleys, hills brown in the summer sun and green in the wet season, the Sierra Nevada towering to the east, rivers that disappeared into the sand by day, giant redwoods in the north —all entranced the travelers. That 500-mile trail from San Diego to Monterey became the *Camino Real*—California's Royal Road.

But when Portolá returned to San Diego, he reported with chagrin that he hadn't found the landlocked harbor. Where it should have been, he saw only a long, open curve in the shore. He kept on searching for a hundred miles north—to the edge of a cliff overlooking a half-mile gap in the shoreline. Powerful ocean currents surged through the gap into an amazingly large inland sea. A foggy, windy place—"the cliffs of the Golden Gate to San Francisco," Dr. Brandes said.

While Portolá and his men debated whether the long bay they had seen really was Monterey, the daily food ration at San Diego dropped to a few bites of tortillas and beans and a few swallows of milk. The Indians, now surly, grew nothing to sell. Floods in the rainy season washed away growing gardens and grain. No supply ship came. Father Serra led daily prayers that San Diego's 100 men would live until help arrived from Mexico. Sixty days later, on March 23, 1770, it seemed a miracle when the sails of the supply ship *San Antonio* came into sight.

Soon, men headed north to build a stick-and-mud fort. By early June any Russian ship trying the long shallow bay that Portolá finally conceded was Monterey would have faced cannon fire. Portolá, his duty done, left on the *San Antonio*.

From the port of San Blas, Mexico, he sent the news to the capital that Alta California was settled. Pleased and smiling, Gálvez and the viceroy joined a procession to a special high Mass in the cathedral while bells pealed and flags fluttered. Probably the Russians would have smiled too had they seen the two dozen soldiers, 50 Mexican Indians, five priests, and a few cannons at each of two flimsy, widely separated presidio-missions guarding all of California.

Between the missions, Father Serra rode on horseback in search of additional sites—good farmland close to large Indian settlements. Within a year and a half he had founded San Carlos Borromeo at Carmelo on the coast near Monterey, San

Antonio de Padua in the mountains south of Monterey, and San Gabriel Arcángel ten miles east of a river now called the Los Angeles.

The wiry ascetic in brown sackcloth robe and sandals flayed himself by night with a barbed lash for sinful thoughts and pleaded by day with the Indians to save their souls by serving the church. Few heeded the call of Serra's mission bells — tied to a tree branch — or were moved by pictures of the Virgin Mary in the brush huts.

But free food brought the Indians to the mission. During 1772, Father Serra and his padres may have given away too much food, for starvation threatened them and the soldiers at Monterey. When the *San Antonio* failed to come, Pedro Fages, Portolá's successor, organized a hunt for the biggest edible animal in California — the grizzly bear. The hunters killed 41 grizzlies, enough to feed his men until pack mules could trudge from San Diego with supplies.

Fages, though tyrannical and bad-mannered, worked with Father Serra in 1772 building the mission of San Luis Obispo de Tolosa in the grizzly hunt area, 125 miles south of Monterey. But soon after, the two men hit an impasse while arguing about how supplies from Mexico should be distributed and about who had authority over converts. Impulsively, Father Serra boarded a ship bound for Mexico. His complaints to the new viceroy, Antonio Bucareli, cost Fages his post.

While in Mexico City, Father Serra also poured out all the bad news about the colony: virtually no supplies, converts, or new settlers during four exhausting years. Bucareli wrote his king to expect an early abandonment of California.

But Father Serra had no intention of giving up. For months he pressed the viceroy. Bucareli listened attentively to his proposals, for Madrid had warned him — as he himself put it — that "His Majesty was in persistent dread of the descent of the Russians." One of Serra's recommendations was to establish an overland route from Mexico's northern provinces to Alta California. "Since Captain Anza, Commandant of Tubac [Sonora] offers to attempt the expedition, I urge Your Excellency to authorize him to do so."

On my way to San Diego, I shuddered as I looked down from jet height over dry, cloudless southern Arizona, once part of Mexico's Sonora province. No green in hundreds of miles of dunes and of red stone ridges and buttes rising from the rock-strewn desert. If Bucareli could have seen what I saw, or if Father Serra had been less desperate, they might never have considered such an undertaking.

But they did. In early 1774, Capt. Juan Bautista de Anza and 34 horsemen rode out of Tubac, a presidio-mission just south of present-day Tucson. They followed Arizona's Gila River west to the Colorado. From there they skirted the vast sand desert now called the Imperial Valley, and climbed north through the San Jacinto Mountains. When on March 22 they ended their long journey at San Gabriel Mission, the friars and soldiers there, as Anza recorded, "could hardly believe that people could have come from Sonora."

Viceroy Bucareli now had an overland trail, and Anza returned on it to Sonora to begin recruiting settlers. Bucareli wanted a large group to start immediately for San Francisco Bay. At Tubac, Anza assembled his group, 240 altogether including three priests. On October 23, 1775, they set out for the California coast. So well organized was Anza that the journey did not cost a single life. Eight children were born on the way. His herders brought more than 1,000 animals. *(Continued on page 178)*

Families from Mexico, led by Juan Bautista de Anza, cross the harsh desert of the Colorado Riv
Basin during their 1,400-mile trek to Monterey. Spurred by fears that Russians planned to

upy Alta California, the expedition set out in October 1775 to build a fort on San Francisco y. At Monterey, Anza turned back. Under José Moraga, the settlers reached the bay in June 1776.

WALTER MEAYERS EDWARDS (BELOW); TOM MYERS

Burros graze at isolated Mission San Antonio de Padua, founded by Father Serra in 1771. Some 70 miles south of Monterey, the restored mission looks much as it did in the late 18th century. For more than a decade Serra administered the Alta California missions from adobe quarters that once stood on the site of San Carlos Borromeo (below) at Carmel. The figure of Saint Francis, founder of the Franciscan Order, now stands inside the church.

As Anza trekked through the mountains toward San Gabriel he was surprised to find that the Indians, previously so friendly, were avoiding him. When he arrived at San Gabriel in January, he learned why. Two months earlier, two hundred converts had joined Indian conspirators at San Diego and killed a priest, Father Jaime. Anza went south with Monterey soldiers to help search out the troublemakers and bring them in to be lashed as punishment. With even more soldiers arriving by ship, the Indians became convinced, as historian Charles E. Chapman writes, "that the Spaniards were coming almost from the skies to punish them." Believing the Spanish invincible, the San Diego Indians never again organized for a large-scale attack.

After rejoining his settlers at San Gabriel, Anza led them north toward San Francisco along the Camino Real. On the seaside plain of present-day Santa Barbara, they passed through a series of 30 villages sheltering 20,000 Indians.

I too followed the Camino Real to Santa Barbara, where my daughter, Suzy, then lived with her husband, Steve Henneman. Together we trailed Anza and his colonists north across the mountains toward Monterey.

In Carmel Valley at Father Serra's home mission, ten miles out of Monterey, we saw the great missionary in marble facing the church's Moorish tower. "But this, like most of California's mission churches, was built much later, and Father Serra never saw it," Suzy remarked. "He said Mass in a simple adobe chapel."

Beyond Carmel, we saw from pine-covered slopes the red tile roofs of Monterey. The blue Pacific was pushing ridges of water against the long curving beach. Anza's people had seen a fort of log-and-mud buildings. Arriving at California's six-year-old capital, "the commander, indeed, had to lodge in the storehouse," a priest wrote, "while the rest of the people accommodated themselves in the plaza with their tents."

The officer in charge of the Alta California troops had no orders from the viceroy, and he refused to let the settlers go on to San Francisco. Anza, ill, angry, and frustrated, left for Sonora, never to return—and never to forget the tearful farewells of settlers he had brought so safely through four danger-filled months.

Viceroy Bucareli's written order, arriving by ship, broke the stalemate at Monterey. "Settle San Francisco," he directed. Anza's lieutenant, José Moraga, left with pack mules and 20 families.

Three miles from San Francisco Bay's sandy beaches, they pitched their tents on fine farmland beside a lagoon named Dolores. In a shelter of branches, Father Pedro Font said Mass on June 29, 1776.

"San Francisco's birth came just six days before the signing of the Declaration of Independence on the other side of the continent," Col. John L. Fellows, Jr., reminded me. Colonel Fellows, the 193rd officer to command the Presidio of San Francisco since Lieutenant Moraga, showed me a neat hole cut through the plaster of the officers' club at this headquarters of the Sixth United States Army. "Deep in there," he said, you can see the original mud brick wall of Moraga's building, built in 1776— the oldest in San Francisco."

A three-mile trail connected the Presidio to the church and mission compound at Dolores lagoon. Compound and pond exist no more, Suzy and I found. But the church, despite earthquakes and time, looks much as it did when its enclosed quadrangle welcomed Indian converts.

Becoming Christians tied the Indians to a disciplined life of hard work. They produced food, clothing, and household goods for the missions, for villages of converts, and for sale to the families in the presidios. Runaway converts were hunted down, whipped, and imprisoned. As Chapman noted, "The missions of Alta California were the richest institutions in the province, virtual owners and managers of a vast economic plant."

But the padres began to object to supplying food and goods to the presidios and being paid in treasury drafts that were never honored. And in Mexico City, officials began to balk at spending money for supply ships for Californians who never sent back anything of value. "What this province needs," wrote Governor Felipe de Neve to Bucareli in 1777, "is farmers in country towns—pueblos—to grow food and herd cattle for presidio people."

Neve wanted one pueblo in the south, at the site of present-day Los Angeles, another in the north. Near the Santa Clara mission the northern pueblo, San José de Guadalupe, was laid out by surveyors. To its vacant fields, Neve sent about 14 families from Monterey and San Francisco.

In Neve's southern pueblo, I strolled with my guide, Carolyn McCulloch, past black-haired, olive-skinned shoppers at stalls in the middle of Olvera Street. "Only Mexico City and Guadalajara have more Mexicans than Los Angeles," Carolyn said. "When Olvera Street and the Old Plaza were restored in the 1930's, it seemed appropriate to turn them into a Little Mexico shopping center. Neve's first settlers here came from Sonora and Sinaloa, the last to follow Anza's trail. They were 11 farmers and their wives—ten Indians, seven mulattoes, two Negroes, a mestizo, and two claiming to be pure Spanish. Not one of them could read or write."

On September 4, 1781, the group walked nine miles west from San Gabriel mission to the newly laid-out square. There they heard an official—perhaps Neve himself—christen it *Pueblo de Nuestra Señora la Reina de Los Angeles,* Village of Our Lady the Queen of the Angels. Each family took possession of a house lot, cattle, tools, seeds, and the month's $10 pay. Padres attending the christening went home shaking their heads at such unpromising people for Los Angeles. Later one wrote, "They pay more attention to gambling and playing the guitar than to tilling their lands and educating their children."

The pueblo settlers marked the end of the new arrivals from New Spain. With the Yuma Indians grown hostile and blocking the Anza Trail, and the Spanish crown unwilling to spend money to send settlers, California found itself cut off. Historian Walton E. Bean of the University of California, Berkeley, notes, "There were about 600 persons [Spanish-Mexicans] in Alta California in 1781, and about five times as many in 1821, but the increase was almost entirely from the birth of descendants of the earlier colonists rather than from the arrival of new ones."

Ironically, corrosion had clogged presidio cannons, and supplies had dropped to one shipload a year, when the Russians, far to the north, began the colony the Spanish had feared 15 years earlier. Perhaps the Russians would have put off a colony even longer if their elegant furs and rich Chinese market had remained a secret.

But the secret began to leak out in 1778 when English explorer James Cook sailed along the shore of the Gulf of Alaska and dropped anchor in harbors from Nootka Sound to the Aleutians. Indians offered furs of a kind new to Cook's men. Warm and silky, they were the Russian American treasure, the sea otter.

Snowy Mount Edgecumbe, ringed in rain clouds and spruce, towers over Kruzof Islan

itka, once Russian Alaska's capital, lines the shore of Baranof Island in the distance.

During much of April in 1778, Nootka Indians a thousand miles north of San Francisco canoed stacks of sea otter pelts to the ships of Captain Cook. Shrewd and light-fingered, they took away knives, chisels, axes, saws. From an earlier Spanish explorer or two they had a few pieces of metal, and they craved more—for weapons, for fishing hooks, for carving wood masks, totem poles, and ceremonial rattles.

Sailing north from Nootka Sound on present-day Vancouver Island, Cook passed hundreds of mountainous, heavily forested islands. Tlingit Indians paddled fur-laden canoes out to his ships to trade. For a thousand miles Cook skirted the northwest coast of America, probing the inlets and bays of a great gulf. Already famous for two Pacific voyages of discovery, he now was seeking a cross-continent waterway to the Atlantic. He also had instructions to find out what the Russians were doing in these parts.

Turning back from narrowing waterways and finally from an impenetrable icepack in the far northern sea, Cook stopped at the Aleutian island of Unalaska. Unexpectedly, an Aleut brought him a gift—a loaf of rye bread and a note in Russian that none in his crew could read. To contact the Russians, Cook sent back with the Aleut an adventurous American, John Ledyard.

Ledyard found Russians, friendly and hospitable, living in temporary half-underground huts of turf and thatch. Three of the Russians returned to the ship with him. To Captain Cook they spoke of the "treacherous Indians" on the mainland, which they called by the Aleut name, *Alashka*. Guardedly, they told him they traded with Aleuts for furs and sold them for modest prices in Siberia.

Months later, after the death of Cook in the Hawaiian Islands, his ships put in at Canton, China. Crew members took their otter skins to the merchants—and gasped when they were paid ten English pounds for a pelt that cost a few pennies' worth of metal. Now they understood what the Russians were really doing: getting rich on Alaskan furs sold in China. The English sailors almost mutinied in a futile effort to force their officers to turn the ships back to Alaska for another load of pelts.

Slowly the news seeped out to other Englishmen, to Americans, and to the French. The escape of the secret dismayed 30-year-old Grigorii Ivanovich Shelikhov, an ambitious fur dealer in Irkutsk, Russia's trading post on the Chinese-Siberian border. Because Czarina Catherine refused to spend a kopeck to protect fur merchant interests, Shelikhov determined he would go into debt to start a year-round settlement to guard Alaska's waters against trespassers. In 1783 he left Siberia and a year later arrived on the southeast coast of Kodiak Island in the Gulf of Alaska.

The island's grassy valleys, emerald green in summer, had changed to a golden October cover when I saw them from Bill Blewett's mail plane. Each day Bill flew the route south from the town of Kodiak, and he knew every ridge, pass, valley, bay, and cove along the island's 100-mile length. We passed four bays, long and narrow like Newfoundland's fjords, before Bill shouted, "That's Three Saints Bay, where the Russians first settled!" On the bay's south shore, at the foot of a wall of low, bare-topped mountains, lay a narrow grassy strip. What it must have cost to supply a colony there, 4,600 miles from its base at Irkutsk!

To Kodiak, Shelikhov brought his vivacious wife, Natalia, and 130 men—a few with wives and children—who had signed to stay five years. In August 1784, they unloaded a small, awkward ship, *Three Saints,* and a sloop.

As the mail plane passed over the site of Shelikhov's village, I thought of how life went for Natalia during her nearly two years in this "factory," as the Russians called such posts. She lived in a hewn-log cabin, one of seven or eight clustered near bunkhouses, offices, storehouses, a sheep and cow barn, and a carpentry shop. Cabbages and potatoes grew well, and salmon packed the streams. Warmed by the Japan Current, the island and nearby mainland coast suffered no harder winters than those of New England.

Soon after arriving at Three Saints Bay, Natalia may have watched her husband teach uncooperative Aleuts a hard lesson. Historian Clarence Andrews records the incident in his book *The Story of Alaska:* "... a large number [of Aleuts] were gathered together on a high, detached rock, off a headland ... where they fancied themselves secure. Shelikhov surrounded them with boats and demanded a surrender. On their refusal he swept the rock with grapeshot from his cannon, and the terrified natives ... plunged headlong into the sea, where many of them [about 400] drowned, and the others were captured by the Russians and held as hostages." Shelikhov needed hundreds of Aleuts to paddle *kayaks* and *baidarkas* — one- and two-man canoes — in the hunt for the sea otter. He also needed Aleuts to prepare the skins in the fur factory.

Eventually, Shelikhov won the Aleuts' loyalty with good treatment and good pay; all summer bowmen in a fleet of 600 baidarkas chased the otter. Indian women lived with the fur hunters, and within the year Aleut-Russian babies cried in Three Saints village. For the older children, Natalia held school.

Shelikhov directed the building of four trading stations on Kodiak. From them he uneasily watched English traders and rival Russians roaming his waters. He needed, he realized, political power as well as settlers to protect his investment. He and Natalia set out for St. Petersburg in 1786 to seek from the Czarina a fur monopoly in Russian America. It took 13 years to get it. Midway, Shelikhov hired Aleksandr Baranov, 43, a hard-driving Siberian fur trader, to go to Kodiak and manage the colony.

As Bill Blewett's seaplane taxied across Kodiak's town harbor, I saw the bright blue domes of the Russian Orthodox Church flashing in the afternoon sun. In front of the church stood a two-story white clapboard house, the Baranov Museum, oldest structure in Alaska.

"Baranov ruled like a czar," Kodiak Islander Liana James told me at the museum, once Baranov's warehouse. "He made Shelikhov's dream of a fur empire come true. In Russian, *baran* means 'wild ram,' a fitting name for a man like Baranov."

Soon after Baranov arrived in 1791, a huge "tidal wave" crashed into the island, washing away most of the buildings at Three Saints. He promptly moved the settlement to the mountain-ringed harbor where the town of Kodiak stands today.

Quickly Baranov learned the dialects of the Aleuts. He reasoned with them, dealt

Overleaf: Tlingits in bright wooden masks storm out of their fort on Sitka as Russians attack the island. The Indians temporarily routed their enemies, killing 10 and wounding 26, including the leader, Aleksandr Baranov (beside cannon). Two years earlier, in 1802, the Tlingits had wiped out a Russian outpost on Sitka, but this time they lost. After enduring heavy cannon fire, they slipped away when their gunpowder supply accidentally exploded.

fairly, paid well. They loved and respected him. On his own men he imposed military discipline, made each stay by only one Aleut woman, and confined their drinking to fermented cranberry juice. On all Russian festival days, he threw a party, enthusiastically joining in the singing and dancing.

To extend his trading posts to the mainland and around to the eastern side of the gulf, he talked the tribal chief of the Tlingit Indians into a peace treaty, sealing it by taking the chief's 18-year-old daughter as his wife. Baranov already had a Russian wife, but he had kept a great distance from her for many years. With the Indian girl, whom he renamed Anna, he lived in a house, now gone, next to the warehouse, Liana James told me. A newly arrived group of eight priests viewed the couple with dismay. But Anna and the two children she bore helped Baranov endure America's dangers, anxieties, hardships, and frustrations for 27 years.

"Both my Russian great-grandfathers helped build this log warehouse for Baranov," retired schoolteacher Eunice Neseth told me. "My great-grandmothers were Aleuts, of course." At the Baranov Museum she showed me samovars, ikons, long Russian pistols, and Aleut stone knives, or *ulu*. Then she brought out a whale gut *kamlaika* — a stiff pullover raincoat — and wriggled into it. "The sea hunter, on his knees in the baidarka, fastened the bottom of his kamlaika around the outside edge of his cockpit," Eunice said. "Then he stayed dry in the roughest weather. And he was safe from drowning because he was an expert at righting his baidarka if it overturned."

Baranov used his kamlaika to deceive his first foreign visitors, Capt. Hugh Moore of the English East India Company and his mate Joseph O'Cain of Boston. Baranov, uncertain whether their ship *Phoenix,* appearing one summer day in 1792, was warship or trader, pulled his kamlaika hood low to shadow his face and paddled a baidarka to its side. He gestured for a rope ladder. On board, the Englishmen led him to trade goods, thinking he was an Aleut. Convinced that *Phoenix* was no warship, Baranov pushed back his hood and laughed at his surprised visitors. That began a long and useful friendship between Baranov and O'Cain.

Both knew German, and talked freely for five days about their business while workers replaced a broken mast. Moore and O'Cain found out how poor and few the Russians were; Baranov learned about the Hawaiians 3,500 miles to the south, who were friendly and had food to sell. He also learned that the English now traded regularly for thousands of furs from the tricky, touchy Tlingits on Sitka — one of Alaska's myriad coastal islands — 600 miles away across the Gulf of Alaska.

Baranov wept when the congenial English served him a good dinner with fresh bread and French wine, the first he'd had in two years. Probably he wept again when Moore and O'Cain departed. But they left him an English teacher, a turbaned Bengalese boy named Richard.

"You can see the English visit in one scene of a play we produce every summer in Kodiak's outdoor theater," Liana James said. Liana is assistant director of "Cry of the Wild Ram," a biography of Baranov written by Alaskan historian Frank Brink. In a clearing among tall spruces on Monashka Bay a few miles outside Kodiak, audiences

Eskimo seal hunter drags his kill across ice floes in the Chukchi Sea off Point Hope, Alaska. To him and his family the seal means food and clothing; in earlier days, furs meant empire and great wealth to the Russian traders.

 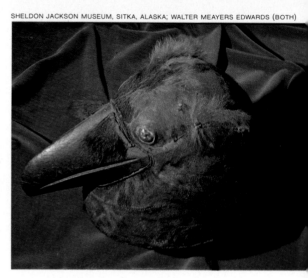

"Land of Russian Possession," proclaims a copper plaque numbered "12" and found in 1935 near Sitka. Russian fur traders buried such markers in Alaska and as far south as California. The Tlingit war leader Katlian wore the raven's head helmet. In bidding farewell to his old enemy Baranov, Katlian said: "Now we are old men together and about to die. Let us be brothers."

of 600 or so crowd simple plank seats in early August. In a setting of forested islands and emerald sea, they watch 150 Kodiak townspeople portray the main characters in Baranov's turbulent career in Alaska: hired artisans and fur hunters... undisciplined serfs, exiles, and criminals... subservient Aleuts... antagonistic priests who convinced Anna to throw Baranov's "child of sin" from a cliff, nearly killing him... English and American traders... arrogant Russian naval officers—who were nobles—lording it over merchant-class Baranov....

During the play, balalaikas strum and church bells ring. Tlingit drums rumble as smoke and fire envelop a new fort started on Sitka—today's Baranof Island. Ship cannons boom, driving away the Tlingits.

Sitka was so rich in sea otter that American, English, and French captains risked their ships and their crews to trade with the mercurial Tlingits.

Baranov knew he must one day settle Sitka to hold Alaska and its otter for Russia. Already English and Spanish interlopers had started forts in Nootka Sound 700 miles south; their kings had nearly gone to war before agreeing to tear down the forts and share the sound for anchorage. In Kodiak's waters and those of the nearby mainland, the arrows of the Aleuts already had killed most of the otter.

"And they would do the same at Sitka," I heard in Kodiak from sea mammal hunter Andre Nault, interrupting a rhapsody about Alaska's wildlife, mountain scenery, and winter sky show of wavering northern lights. "In fact, from the Aleutians to California, the sea otter would all but disappear," he said. But it was the Americans, I reminded him, who brought them to the vanishing point after the United States purchased Alaska in 1867. "Well, since 1911 there's been a heavy fine for killing one, and now our waters have up to 125,000 otters. I see them everywhere."

In 1799, Baranov decided the time had come to occupy Sitka, for Tlingits on the island were acquiring guns from English and American traders. With a thousand Indian allies in baidarkas and a hundred Russian settlers in three small ships, Baranov crossed the Gulf of Alaska from Kodiak.

"At first, he had little trouble starting a settlement here," Superintendent Daniel Kuehn told me at the National Park Service Headquarters in the town of Sitka. We rode six miles to Old Sitka, where Baranov built a fort beside a broad meadow crossed by a swift salmon stream. "Friendship with a chief and Baranov's good sense and forceful courage controlled the Tlingits for the 18 months or so he stayed. But in June of 1802, about a year after he went back to Kodiak, a war party of Tlingits burned the fort, killing most of the settlers, taking but a few captive," Dan said. In all, some 200 Aleuts and Russians died in the attack.

When the news reached Kodiak, Baranov was at a peak in his career. A messenger from St. Petersburg, 7,000 hazardous miles away, earlier had handed Baranov a letter that had taken him three years to deliver. The letter said Shelikhov's widow and her son-in-law Count Nikolai Rezanov, a court minister, had in 1799 gained a fur monopoly from Czar Paul I. Manager Baranov was now Governor Baranov. Along with valuable shares in the company, they sent him a citation "for faithful service in hardship and want and for unremitting loyalty." Again, Baranov wept.

Kodiak's biggest party and dance were followed by its deepest gloom when Sitka's few survivors arrived with their terrible news. They came with an English sea captain who had captured them from the Tlingits — and he extracted a high ransom from Baranov for their return.

For two years Baranov's anger smoldered against the Tlingits on Sitka. But he had too little ammunition and arms to conquer those pale-brown people, so hardy they could walk barefoot on ice and snow. At last, in 1804, his Bostonian friend O'Cain brought the guns and powder Baranov had ordered the year before when O'Cain called at Kodiak and provided the Russians with desperately needed goods from his own ship's stores. To pay for the battle supplies, Baranov let O'Cain borrow 60 Aleuts and their baidarkas for the first of a long series of Russian-Yankee otter poaching forays into the Spanish waters of California.

With 800 Aleuts in baidarkas hovering about four ships, Baranov and 120 Russians set out for Sitka, where he discovered he had unexpected help — a Russian frigate, the *Neva*. Capt. Yurii Lisianskii had heard in Hawaii about the Sitka war, news brought earlier by O'Cain. Lisianskii hurried north to help against the *koloshi* as the Russians called the Indians. A *koluschan* was the disk of wood worn by Tlingit women of rank to distend the lower lip into a duckbill shape.

When the Tlingits saw the attackers, they quickly left their village for a log fort a mile down the shore. Baranov landed a force and occupied their abandoned town, atop a rocky knoll now called Castle Hill. He demanded surrender of the fort. The Tlingits refused.

On Castle Hill, as I read Lisianskii's account of the battle, I looked out over the bay toward jagged stone mountains laced with light October snow and ribboned with fog. Dark green spruce forests mantled lower hills and the bay shore. I visualized the fleet of baidarkas tugging the Russian ships into position off a point of land.

The ships bombarded the fort, and Baranov sent a small force to destroy the Tlingit canoes on the beach and set fire to a nearby barn. He then led a landing force of 150 men to the attack. As the invaders rushed ashore, the Tlingits charged them, yelling and firing flintlocks. Thrown into disorder as companions fell dead or screamed in pain, Russians and Aleuts ran back to their boats.

"The Tlingits say only one man, their war leader Katlian, went out to face the attackers," Dan Kuehn said. "An old Indian told me the Tlingit version of the battle. On the morning of October 1, Katlian put on the great clan helmet, in the shape of a raven's head, and armed himself with a blacksmith's hammer he'd acquired in the destruction of Old Sitka fort. Hidden by a floating log, he glided around the point of the little peninsula. When the invaders landed, Katlian jumped up and ran toward them, screaming and swinging the hammer. Frightened Aleuts and Russians turned back to their boats. Tlingits inside the fort opened fire. Ten men fell dead. Twenty-six more were wounded, Baranov among them. Katlian is still a great hero among the Tlingits, and the helmet and hammer have been preserved."

When the land attack failed, Lisianskii took over command from the wounded Baranov, moved the ships closer to shore, and began bombarding the fort again. "After four days, the Tlingits suffered a critical blow," Dan related. "I once heard two aged women sing a tribal song that describes what happened. A canoe bringing all their gunpowder from an island cache blew up when a spark from a flintlock set off a keg of gunpowder. Now the Tlingits were defenseless. On the sixth day, the Russians prepared for an assault, possibly thinking they would soon capture a thousand new servants. But during the night, the Tlingits slipped into the woods. Next morning the Russians found in the fort only a few dead children killed by the Tlingits themselves. Perhaps they feared the cries of the children would give away the escape route."

"But we never surrendered," the Tlingits still say. Even today they consider themselves above the Aleuts the Russians enslaved.

Despite surly Tlingits drifting back to Sitka, despite hunger, scurvy, unruly fur hunters, and insubordinate naval officers, Baranov built a Russian American capital, the continent's west coast commercial center for half a century.

He even dared to send a trading ship to San Francisco the year after taking Sitka. Unseasonal storms and fear of the Tlingits had stopped hunting and fishing; the food situation became desperate. Count Rezanov, who was visiting Baranov on Sitka, sailed to the Golden Gate to buy wheat, beans, and meat from the Dolores presidio-mission. At first the Spanish commandant refused. But when Rezanov, now a widower, and the commandant's 17-year-old daughter Doña Concepción Argüello fell in love, the commandant approved their betrothal and agreed to sell the food. A few months after departing, Rezanov died while on his way to St. Petersburg to seek permission to wed his Spanish sweetheart, a Roman Catholic. The waiting girl learned of his death 36 years later.

While the Spanish at four presidios tried to warn away foreigners with their impressive looking if useless cannons, Baranov ceremoniously greeted all ships calling at Sitka, 2,000 miles north of San Francisco. He needed their food and equipment. American traders, including ship owner John Jacob Astor, organizer of fur trapping in Oregon country, began to supply Baranov regularly. In exchange, Baranov loaned them Aleuts and baidarkas to poach California sea otter. They sold Baranov's share of pelts under the American trade privileges at Canton.

Still, Baranov wanted a dependable, Russian source for wheat and vegetables to supply Sitka. In 1812, he sent 95 men to start a farm settlement in warmer land to the south — California. *(Continued on page 196)*

"We no sooner drew near the inlet than we found the coast to be inhabited,"
wrote Captain Cook in his account of Nootka Sound, on today's Vancouver
Island. "Our arrival [in 1778] brought a great concourse of natives [Nootka
Indians] to our ships.... We soon discovered that they were as light-fingered as
any of our friends in the islands we had visited." Of a Nootka house Cook
wrote: "On the inside, one may see from one end to the other without
interruption ... many are decorated with images ... the trunks of very large
trees ... set up singly or by pairs with the front carved into a human face."

NATIONAL MARITIME MUSEUM OF GREENWICH (TOP); PEABODY MUSEUM, HARVARD UNIVERSITY

"Next to a beautiful young woman, a prime sea otter skin ... is the finest natural object in the world," rhapsodized a Yankee ship captain. Indeed, its highly prized fur brought the Pacific sea otter almost to extinction. Sea mammal pelts, including those of sea lions (right), first sparked Russian interest in Alaska. Spanish, French, English, and New England fur traders also hunted the Gulf of Alaska and the waters off the mainland coast as far south as California. Much of the treasure in furs went to China, where the Manchu upper class paid high prices. Protected by law, sea otters now thrive, with as many as 125,000 living in Alaska's waters and another 2,000 off northern California. Below, a sea otter eats a freshly caught crab while floating on its back.

M. L. JOHNSON (ABOVE); TOMAS SENNETT

"There is a great abundance of these trees . . . named redwood for their color," wrote missionary Jua

TOM MYERS

respí of California's coastal giants. In 1774 Spanish sea captains explored as far north as Canada.

I drove for four hours along California's coastal heights and ravines from San Francisco to Russian Fort Ross, 90 winding miles north from the Golden Gate. By sea a sailing ship with a fair wind and moderate seas could make it in about 24 hours —a disturbing thought for the Spanish.

High above the Pacific on a field of shimmering green grass, I climbed a watchtower at the restored palisaded fort. Small cannons in those towers were kept in working order; but the only Spaniards who came near were seeking to trade cattle and horses for such goods as bricks and shoe leather. They took back to San Francisco the news that the Russians had window glass, a piano, and French wine.

In 1841, with Alaska's profits turned to debts, the Russians sold 29-year-old Fort Ross to a rancher, John Sutter, whose millstream nuggets were soon to set off California's gold rush.

Baranov had been gone from Alaska for more than two decades. In 1818, old and sick, he had said goodbye to Sitka Tlingits long since reconciled to the Russians' presence and now lining the shore where Baranov's ship awaited him. Katlian was there. But for a reason unknown to historians, it was to another Indian that Baranov presented a shirt of mail he had worn for protection against the Indians. Aboard ship on the way home, the worn-out czar of Russian America died and was buried at sea.

In Alaska, Baranov's son-in-law, the temporary governor, and Baranov's daughter Irina took a census of the empire her father had built. They counted 399 Russians. Half of them, including 11 women, lived on Sitka. There Baranov's successors took over a house furnished with oil paintings, costly furniture, ornaments, and a large library—a proper setting for a spirited social life that continued another 50 years, with music and dancing, silken gowns and royal governors.

At dawn, I stood on Sitka's Castle Hill, where Baranov once lived, and watched as an unseen sun behind the mountains flicked rosy light onto a scattering of clouds. The sea slowly took on a tinge of pink; morning's first rays glinted copper on the onion-shaped church dome in the middle of the little town. At least the Wild Ram had an enchanting view to begin each tempestuous day.

On other coasts, I had heard California mission bells, walked once-bloody Florida dunes, hunched through the hold of the *Mayflower* in Massachusetts, fished in Newfoundland. On the rocky knoll at Sitka, I thought with awe of the vast spectacle, the ambitious, vigorous Europeans on the continent's shores, praying at first for riches and miracles, then changing habits and character to stay alive in the primitive land. Its dangers demanded courage and quick action; its remoteness and wilderness imposed poverty, a whiplash for labor and discipline. But the woodman's unfettered life in America transformed his spirit. As a landowner he felt equal to landlords in Europe, and in 1776 his descendants let them know it. John Adams later observed that "the real American Revolution" was not the war itself but "the revolution in the minds and hearts of the people . . . radical change in their principles, opinions, sentiments, and affections."

After journeying around the perimeter of our country to gather the stories of settlements along the wild shores, I knew that the radical change Adams spoke of began the day the settlers first set foot on the continent. And I understood as I never had before how much the American spirit that is our heritage bears the imprint of the hard but spacious wilderness.

Russians in California till fields around Fort Ross, built 90 miles north of San Francisco in 1812. Here they hoped to grow food for settlements in Alaska. Though the Spanish king claimed all of California, his subjects there traded at Fort Ross for such necessities as brick and tile, rope, barrels, kegs, and leather (emerging from a tanning vat below).

Restored Fort Ross, now a state historic park, stands on a bluff overlooking the Pacific. The fort takes its name from Rossiia, or Russia. A Russian Orthodox chapel forms part of the log palisade. The original structure collapsed during an earthquake in 1906. Russia, her southward expansion stopped by the Monroe Doctrine of 1823, sold Fort Ross in 1841 to California rancher John Sutter.

*A*merica, her diverse people tested and proved in the crucible of an inhospitable wilderness, slowly came of age to take her place among the world's nations — self-reliant, even defiant. Her early history a reflection of European rivalries and antagonisms, her fabric woven of many strands, she emerged free and strong, the realization of many aspirations. From Plymouth to St. Augustine, from Sitka to San Diego, a new society had been born in the vastness of a nearly empty continent.

TOM MYERS

Boldface indicates illustrations; *italic* refers to picture captions.

ACKNOWLEDGMENTS

The Special Publications Division is grateful to the individuals, organizations, and agencies named or quoted in the text and to those cited here for their generous cooperation and assistance during the preparation of this book: consultants at the California Department of Parks and Recreation, Embassy of Canada, Embassy of Mexico, Jamestown Foundation, Plimoth Plantation, Sitka Historical Society, Smithsonian Institution, The South Carolina Historical Society; and Mrs. Fred Morrison and Harold L. Peterson.

Reproductions of the John White drawings have been made from the Page-Holgate facsimiles, Collection of the L. R. Wilson Memorial Library, The University of North Carolina, by permission of the University of North Carolina Press.

ADDITIONAL READING

The reader may want to check the *National Geographic Index* for related articles, and to refer to the following books:

Charles M. Andrews, *The Colonial Period of American History,* Vols. I-III; Clarence L. Andrews, *The Story of Alaska;* Matthew Page Andrews, *History of Maryland;* Edward Arber, *The Story of the Pilgrim Fathers;* Philip L. Barbour, *Pocahontas and Her World;* John K. Bettersworth, *Mississippi: A History;* H. P. Biggar, *Voyages of Jacques Cartier;* Herbert E. Bolton and Mary Ross, *The Debatable Land;* Herbert E. Bolton, *Fray Juan Crespí;* J. M. S. Careless, *Canada, A Story of Challenge;* John A. Caruso, *The Southern Frontier;* E. Keble Chatterton, *Captain John Smith;* Dwight B. Heath, ed., *Russian America;* R. V. Coleman, *The First Frontier;* Converse Clowse, *Economic Beginnings in Colonial South Carolina;* E. Merton Coulter, *Georgia, a Short History;* Verner W. Crane, *The Southern Frontier;* John T. Cunningham, *New Jersey, America's Main Road;* Edwin A. Davis, *Louisiana, a Narrative History;* Omer Englebert, *The Last of the Conquistadors, Junípero Serra;* Federal Writers' Project, *Rhode Island, a Guide to the Smallest State;* John Fiske, *The Dutch and Quaker Colonies in America,* Vols. I-II; James R. Gibson, *Feeding the Russian Fur Trade;* Clayton C. Hall, *Narratives of Early Maryland;* Dwight B. Heath, ed., *A Journal of the Pilgrims at Plymouth, Mourt's Relation;* Henry F. Howe, *Prologue to New England;* J. Franklin Jameson, *Narratives of New Netherland;* Katherine M. Jones, *Port Royal Under Six Flags;* Aurel Krause, *The Tlingit Indians;* John Lankford, ed., *Captain John Smith's America;* Hugh T. Lefler and Albert R. Newsome, *The History of a Southern State, North Carolina;* Marc Lescarbot, *Nova Francia;* Samuel E. Morison, *Builders of the Bay Colony,* and *Samuel de Champlain, Father of New France;* John E. Pomfret, *Colonial New Jersey;* Daniel W. Prowse, *History of Newfoundland;* Charles B. Reed, *The First Great Canadian;* Thomas L. Stokes, *The Savannah;* Rev. Henry O. Thayer, *The Sagadahoc Colony;* Marcel Trudel, *The Beginnings of New France;* Albert E. Van Dusen, *Connecticut;* Alden T. Vaughan, *New England Frontier;* David D. Wallace, *The History of South Carolina;* George F. Willison, *Saints and Strangers;* James G. Wilson, *The Memorial History of the City of New-York;* Justin Winsor, *The Memorial History of Boston;* John Winthrop, *Winthrop's Journal;* Louis B. Wright, *The Atlantic Frontier;* John H. Wuorinen, *The Finns on the Delaware.*

Library of Congress ⊂⫯P Data

Snell, Tee Loftin.
 The Wild Shores: America's Beginnings
 1. America—Discovery and exploration.
2. United States—History—Colonial
period, ca. 1600-1775. 3. United States—
History—1783-1865. I. National
Geographic Society, Washington, D. C.
Special Publications Division. II. Title.
III. America's beginnings.
E121.S63   973.1   74-1564
ISBN 0-87044-148-5

Composition for this book by National Geographic's Photographic Services, Carl M. Shrader, Director, Lawrence F. Ludwig, Assistant Director. Printed and bound by Holladay-Tyler Printing Corp., Rockville, Md. Color separations by Colorgraphics, Inc., Beltsville, Md.; Graphic Color Plate, Inc., Stamford, Conn.; Graphic South, Charlotte, N.C.; Progressive Color Corp., Rockville, Md.; and J. Wm. Reed Co., Alexandria, Va.

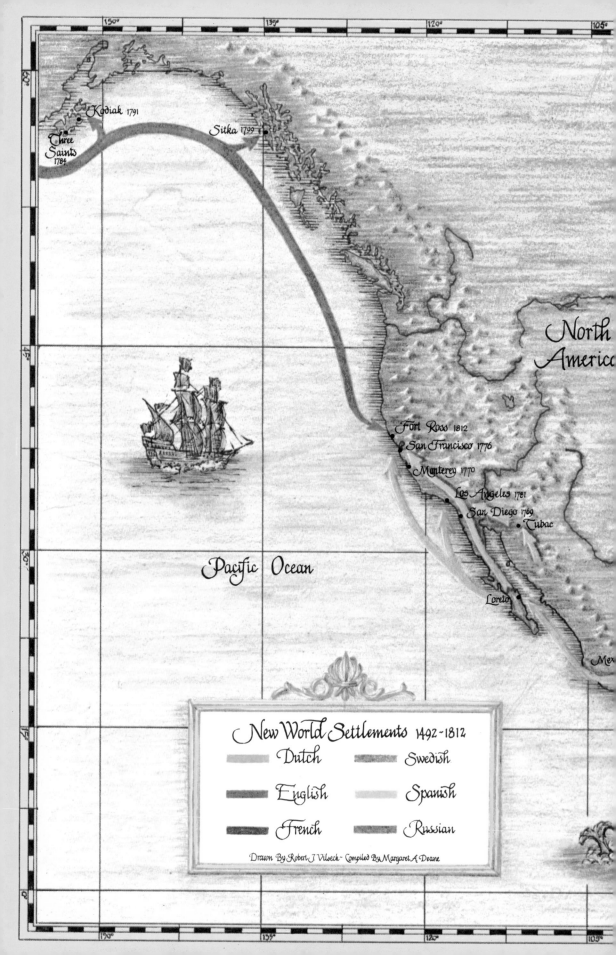

Kodiak 1791

Sitka 1799

Three
Saints
1784

North
America

Fort Ross 1812
San Francisco 1776
Monterey 1770
Los Angeles 1781
San Diego 1769
Tubac

Loreto

Mex

Pacific Ocean

New World Settlements 1492-1812

Dutch   Swedish

English   Spanish

French   Russian

Drawn By Robert J Vilseck ~ Compiled By Margaret A Deane